PRAISE FOR *THE CC*

MW00851738

"Educators understand the
We know how vital it is to
sometimes we forget that climate and culture truly starts in the
classroom. The relationships our students have with each other will
make or break their school year. I love the way Trevor encourages
educators to develop a classroom environment centered around
collaborative work with peers. A collaborative classroom allows
for positive climate and culture, not only for educators but also
for children. If you want to see positive climate and culture in the
classroom, this book is a great place to start."

—**Gerry Brooks,** elementary principal,
author of *Go See the Principal*

"*The Collaborative Classroom*—the title alone has me intrigued. Not
only am I the dean of a school chain with 14,000 students enrolled,
I am also the parent of a 7-year-old little girl. My need for Trevor's
book runs deep and profound. I have often felt sorry for the
smartest, most talented people, who rely solely on their own gifts,
because collaboration is such a beautiful thing. *The Collaborative
Classroom* is a practical guide for teaching all students—whether
in a K-12, college, or beauty school-—to combine their gifts and
successfully collaborate. Trevor is a 'thought you might like to know'
storyteller who delivers his message with conviction and grace."

—**Winn Claybaugh,** founder and dean of Paul Mitchell Schools

"Collaboration is a topic that we know is key to successful
interactions and higher-level problem solving, and yet often
we take for granted how to make this happen. Trevor skillfully
provides the blueprint for intentional teaching of collaboration
skills by sharing a repertoire of strategies, resources, and tools
that are eminently practical and yield a higher level of problem
solving. His thought-provoking questions on reflection and take-
action steps for each chapter are meaningful and inspirational.
This is a must-read for any teacher or administrator who needs a
framework for implementing collaboration in schools and believes
in the power of interdependence in a team."

—**Kim Austin,** principal of Kate Waller Barrett Elementary School

"Collaboration, one of the most important 'soft' skills needed in today's world, requires intentional planning and preparation. In this book, Trevor provides practical tips and advice that any teacher can put to immediate use in the classroom. I especially appreciated his suggestions for managing and assessing collaborative learning activities and his perspective on when collaboration may NOT be the appropriate choice. Conversational and easy to read, this text will be inspirational to both novice and experienced teachers!"

—**Dr. Susan English**, dean of education, Aquinas College

"Hold up, is there a rooftop to shout from nearby? I am AMAZED over what a tremendous resource and wealth of knowledge *The Collaborative Classroom* provides. As an elementary PBL teacher, I know firsthand the importance of real-world learning that is taught and inspired in the classroom. I cannot preach loudly enough that collaboration is a key to problem solving and the process of innovation—a topic often skipped in college classes. I am amazed at how Trevor takes this idea and teaches us with intention and relatable authenticity. He understands the challenges that teachers face, yet provides ideas and skills that are easily adaptable to the elementary classroom. He advances the idea of collaboration as a brick that should be laid for the foundation of success, a culture of community, and a framework of achievement through the lens of real-world learning. Trevor provides tools that can be brought back to the classroom to help create a culture of change that feeds out of the hands of collaboration to constructively change the dynamic of our students' lives, our schools and, most importantly, our world. As educators, the future is in OUR hands, and *The Collaborative Classroom* teaches us one way to take charge and make it a better today!"

—**Julia Graeser,** elementary teacher

"Trevor has a gift for storytelling and drawing students into the learning zone of collaboration. The idea of group work can cause anxiety on the part of many teachers and students. *The Collaborative Classroom* is essential in guiding students to success now and in the workplace. Trevor takes readers through the process of involving all students and offers a treasure chest of resources to assist you on the journey of meaningful, purposeful, and lasting student collaboration!"

—Dr. Dorothy VanderJagt, founder of iFireUP

"Trevor Muir has produced something here that is definitely not a typical educational read. From the opening of the introduction, one cannot stop thinking, feeling, laughing, and contemplating how Trevor could be this honest. But he is. He speaks openly, candidly, and considerately on how we can make school better for all of our students, no matter what type of learners they are, if we are just more thoughtful in how we establish our classrooms and collaborative activities. The creative ideas and resources Trevor includes are ones that any teacher could add to their repertoire. Similar to *The Epic Classroom,* every idea Trevor shares he explains through a story to keep every reader engaged throughout. This is an "education book" that reads like fiction, which will soon become one of your most highlighted, tattered, referenced resources. Thank you, as always, Trevor, for sharing your personal thoughts, failures, and successes so we too can have a rewarding, epic classroom."

—Martin Geoghegan, elementary principal and former president of Massachusetts ASCD

"Trevor Muir has crafted a practical guide that helps teachers tackle one of the biggest challenges they face: how to cultivate meaningful collaboration. As a master storyteller, he shares powerful examples of what happens when teachers take collaboration to the next level with their students."

—John Spencer, professor and author of *Launch* and *Empower*

"Some skills are innate, and some can be taught, then honed with practice, and developed into an area of expertise. Luckily for his students, and now for his readers, Trevor has used his skill of insight to analyze how students, and really all humans, react and interact with each other. He has managed to use this insight to break down the classroom dynamic—analyzing concepts such as collaboration, criticism techniques, and accountability that play into all classroom activity. After dissecting them, he builds on them, bringing us to a body of knowledge useful not only in the educational sphere, or the workplace, but even in family relationships. His words constantly make me think of how I can employ his techniques and suggestions. I found myself wanting to jot down portions that intrigued and spoke to me. This book would be a useful handbook for any educator concerned about effective communication in their classroom."

—Janice Choinere, veteran teacher

"Trevor's real stories combined with hands-on work makes this book an attractive whole for me. As a reader (and teacher), you will recognize yourself in many situations. That also gives me a kind of peace and self-confidence—there are more people who, like me, experience difficult moments in the classroom."

—Jochem Goedhals, director of Fontys University PULSED

"Trevor Muir presents humor, personal classroom experiences, and enthusiasm throughout this book. He gives straightforward and helpful information through humor and by sharing his personal classroom experiences of both success and failure. As a veteran teacher often overwhelmed by new ideas, this book provided me with an innovative look at creating a successful collaborative classroom. As I read, I found the Reflections and Take Action parts at the end of each chapter to be beneficial as I thought of my current classrooms and my goals for them. I am motivated to implement many of the ideas as soon as possible. Thank you, Trevor Muir, for helping us create successful collaboration in classrooms in any grade."

—Donna Beers, teacher

The COLLABORATIVE CLASSROOM

Teaching Students How to *Work Together Now* and for the *Rest of Their Lives*

TREVOR MUIR

This book is available at special discounts when purchased in quantity for use as premiums, promotions, fundraisers, or for educational use. For inquiries and details, contact the publisher at books@daveburgessconsulting.com.

Published by Dave Burgess Consulting, Inc.
San Diego, CA
DaveBurgessConsulting.com

Cover Design by Dave Battjes and Genesis Kohler
Editing and Interior Design by My Writers' Connection
Interior Illustrations by Sarah DeBaar

Library of Congress Control Number: 2019954768
Paperback ISBN: 978-1-951600-00-6
Ebook ISBN: 978-1-951600-01-3

First Printing: November 2019

DEDICATION

When I was in fourth grade, my teacher assigned the class a project over Thanksgiving where each student had to demonstrate their understanding of Western Expansion and the pioneers. I thought I'd just do my research by playing Oregon Trail, scribble some pictures with colored pencils, and call it a day. My mom had other ideas. She suggested I write a whole book and that we bind it with cowhide leather and burn the title into the cover with a soldering iron.

I pushed back hard against this idea, as I wanted to spend my Thanksgiving Break playing and not working on a dumb book, but my mother wasn't having any of that. For the next seven days, we sat down at her 1994 Compaq computer and collaborated to write and create my first book. (Don't worry, she let me play during the break as well.)

When I turned in the final project, I felt I had created a masterpiece. My teacher told me I was a real author. My book told me I was a real author. And my mom told me I was a real author. I believed all of them and have been writing ever since.

So this book is dedicated to my mama, who has never let me settle for scribbled drawings and always encouraged me to write the book.

CONTENTS

THE NEED FOR A COLLABORATIVE CLASSROOM

Alone we can do so little;
together we can do so much.

—Helen Keller

When I was a freshman in college, my humanities professor assigned the class a group project. We were told to form groups of four and complete the team assignment on our own time before the next class meeting. He said the grade for this project would be a portion of our final and that everyone in the group would receive the same grade. He explained the instructions, presented the rubric he would use to assess our work, and then dismissed the class.

My first thought was, *Wait a minute. Isn't he going to assign our groups?*

Looking around at the large college class, I realized I didn't know a single person in the room. It wasn't like high school, where I'd been only months before and had some type of acquaintance with everyone in all of my classes. My anxiety rose as I tried to make eye contact with another student in the room to start a group. Nobody would meet my eye, and it seemed like all the other students already knew each other well, and I was just this strange loner awkwardly pacing the lecture hall.

Just as I was about to approach the professor and ask him whether I could complete the assignment on my own, I felt a tap on my shoulder. I turned and saw three girls smiling at me, and the one who tapped me said, "Hi, do you want to be in our group? We're going to work on it tonight."

Struggling mightily to form actual words, I eventually managed to croak, "Y-y-yes."

It was like divine intervention. These girls wanted *me* to be in their group and extended an invite to come to their apartment that evening to work together.

We're definitely not in high school anymore, Toto.

After fumbling through an introduction, I offered to pick up the project supplies before coming over. That night I arrived at the apartment in my just-washed cargo shorts and wearing my favorite pooka-shell necklace. While I was prepared to work on the project, I was even more excited by the fact that they chose me to be in their group and that I might actually make friends in college.

I walked through the door with a poster board and markers in my hand, and instead of, "Hey you! So glad you're here!" one of the girls said, "Hey, do you mind if our boyfriends hang out while we work on this?"

Boyfriends?

"Umm, sure," I said.

And that was about it for the group project.

For an hour that evening, I worked on the project by myself in the living room of three strangers while they laughed, talked, and watched TV with their boyfriends. I finally told them I'd just take the project home with me and finish it by the due date. All of my "group mates" said that was so sweet of me and to let them know what they could do to help.

A couple days—and hours of work later—I submitted the project. My professor awarded me—and each of the members of my group—an A. It didn't matter that I had done all the work. The professor didn't take into account the money I spent on supplies, my hours of research, or that the other group mates watched *Dawson's Creek* while I drew graphs on a poster board. We all received the same grade.

To add insult to injury, the professor publicly commended our group in front of the class for the beautiful and thorough project. I faked a smile while my three group mates put on very real ones.

From that day forward, I joined the massive contingent of people—teachers, students, and professionals alike—who hate group projects.

Collaboration Is an Essential Skill

Thinking back on this story, I realize there are many things I could have done differently during my first-ever college group project. I could have sought out people to be in a group with rather than desperately saying yes while hoping to make friends or score a date.

I could have asked my partners to turn off the television and help me research.

I could have suggested we meet at the school library.

When asked to do the lion's share of the work, I could have simply said, "No."

I could have made a spreadsheet listing every group member's tasks.

I could have sent text messages to the other group members asking for project status updates.

I could have held a serious conversation with anyone who wasn't doing their share and asked them whether they wanted to leave the group if they didn't want to contribute.

I could have collaborated.

The truth is, however, I didn't know how to do any of that. The bulk of my education career up to that point had been an individual operation. Aside from the rare group assignment in which students usually had to create a PowerPoint presentation—which mostly entailed every person completing a different slide and pasting them into the same presentation with different fonts, styles, and levels of detail—I had very little exposure to quality group work.

So much of my education experience growing up was spent sitting in rows and learning information so that I could complete an assignment, pass a test, or learn and grow. School was about personal growth and achievement, and that makes perfect sense. School is often framed as a place to grow the individual. Stanford Professor David Labaree,[1] in his research paper "Public Goods, Private Goods: The American Struggle over Educational Goals," argues that one of the chief goals of the American education system, for better or for worse, is social mobility. School is essentially an extension of capitalism. It exists so that those who succeed in it can live fruitful and fulfilling lives, attaining their desired social standing. Social mobility asks the question: "What can school do for me, regardless of what it can do for others?" It's a race to the top (sound familiar?), with students and educators having the aim of winning. This comes in the form of grades, promotion, college degrees, and eventually good jobs.

The purpose of school is most often to serve the individual, and pedagogy is designed accordingly. Classroom seating, for instance, is usually arranged for the individual. When a kid sits at a single desk oriented toward the front of the room, it is so the instructor can personally teach them. Standardized tests measure individual growth. Kids who excel are put in honors courses to advance further and faster. In these honors classes, the work often becomes even more about the individual and less about the collective.

Many could form a strong argument that social mobility is the best and most appropriate goal for education. The more individuals excel and rise to the top, the more people can attain their goals and live happier lives. Such an objective certainly has merit and has worked for a lot of people for a long time, even if it does leave out the fact that when there are winners, there must also be losers. And in an ideal society, the education system would be designed so that no child is left behind (I bet that sounds familiar as well).

Let's assume for a minute that social mobility, helping individuals achieve success, is the correct purpose for education and best overall for society. Is the style of learning we see most commonly in schools the optimal way for students to achieve success? Is a predominantly individual-oriented education actually most beneficial to the learner? Is placing students in rows by themselves, valuing only assignments completed by individuals, and making students take assessments that solely measure individual growth the best way to grow a student's capabilities and prepare them to rise to the top in our modern society?

I would argue that it does not.

The problem with the individual focus of school is that it leaves the learner lacking that absolutely essential skill of collaboration when they finish their education. Collaboration is a skill required by all levels of industry in the constantly modernizing twenty-first century, a competency that was not nearly as vital during the industrial twentieth century. A LinkedIn survey of more than two thousand business leaders showed that most employers would rather hire people with collaborative skills than with hard skills specific to that industry. Collaboration is growing only more crucial as the world continues to develop and change.

Even if the purpose of education is to get *everyone* to rise to the top (what Labaree calls "democratic equality") an individual focus still falls short. That's because collaboration is essential not only to individual success but also to moving society forward.

It was the skill of collaboration—that ability to work with others, communicate, problem-solve, give critical feedback, brainstorm, and not lose our minds in the process to successfully produce a specific outcome—that I needed in my freshman year of college when three pretty girls made me do their homework.

Notice how I didn't call collaboration a trait or attribute. It is a skill, just as reading, writing, shooting a basketball, computer programming, or operating a machine are skills. We are not born with the innate ability to collaborate. Working together is advantageous, but people have to learn how to do it and how to do it well.

The modern workforce requires that people grasp this skill. Whether they work for an open-space tech company or even in a modern factory, people must know how to solve problems and achieve goals by working together. In a 2015 article for *Work Design Magazine*, Markku Allison,[2] a thought leader on architecture and design, said that in today's workplace "almost any project of any type or scope is now a complex challenge, as opposed to just simple or complicated. The number of moving parts and players contributing to decisions is great." Because of how connected everything is in the twenty-first century, he said, complex problem solving is required, and it's best accomplished through collaboration.

Colleges and universities are demanding more and more collaboration from current and prospective students. Industry is begging K–12 education to emphasize collaboration so students can excel in the modern workforce. The political world desperately needs people who know how to collaborate and work together (Can I get an amen?). Yet the American education system continues to do very little to teach this increasingly critical skill.

Teaching Collaboration Is Difficult

With this book, I am building a case for why schools must steer away from the constant individual focus and instead build a collaborative foundation. I am also prepared for the eye rolls and pushback:

Yeah, I get it, kids need to learn how to collaborate. They tell us this at staff meetings all the time, but, clearly, you've never tried to get thirty twelve-year-olds to work together in groups.

You must have never had to prepare your students for standardized tests.

You don't know what it's like to have students who sit in rows in all of their other classes walk like zombies into yours and have no interest in working with others.

You must have never had to deal with a parent who freaked out because their kid got the same grade as everyone else in their group.

You've never had a principal who wants quiet and hyper-controlled classrooms.

The list goes on. To be honest, I have experienced all of these situations. I still have nightmares from the first time I tried group work with middle schoolers. I totally get the pushback.

Collaboration is difficult. Teaching collaboration—and making group projects genuinely meaningful—is extremely difficult. There's assigning groups, scheduling work time, and assessing students individually. It's challenging to move a group of students out of an individual mindset and into a group mindset. It's also tricky finding ways to prevent slackers from pulling a group down or bossy take-over students from doing all the work.

What often happens is that many educators remember how much they disliked group work in high school or college and swear they'll never force that on their own students. Or maybe they actually try it, only to crash and burn, leaving their students in sheer dread of the next collaborative activity.

In my first year of teaching, I had an idea for a group project that I thought would blow the doors off of my classroom. In groups of four, my students would interview actual World War II veterans and record the interviews with their parents' cameras. They would take the footage and create documentaries to air at a local theater for the veterans, their families, and the rest of the community to see. My students, who were high school freshmen, would not learn about World War II from a textbook; they would get their information from people who'd actually experienced it.

I was a first-year teacher with stars in my eyes. What could possibly go wrong?

After preparing for the interviews, we piled onto a bus and went to a local retirement home to meet the veterans. When we arrived, I learned that half of the veterans were sick and would not be able to participate. I thought, "No problem, I'll just combine groups and have groups of eight interview each veteran."

Because what could possibly go wrong with putting my students in groups of eight?

Although the rooms were a little more crowded than I intended, and some kids could not see the interviews live and had to wait out in hallways, we captured the veterans' stories and brought the footage back to school to create the documentaries.

That's when the chaos ensued. It turns out only one person can really work on editing a video at a time. Most of the students played nose-goes or rock-paper-scissors, and one unlucky student was given the role of editor and had to sit at the computer poring over an hour of footage. I tried to think of other tasks everyone else could do, such as finding b-roll footage or creating subtitles, but those tasks quickly ran out, and the kid who drew the short straw continued doing the bulk of the work.

After several days of this, the class started veering out of control. I learned quickly that ninth graders with nothing to do can lead to pandemonium. We hadn't covered that in teacher college! Kids were playing pranks on each other and running around the classroom. Some started working on homework from other classes. Others snuck out and began wandering around school, only to get walked back to my class by the principal, who asked me how they left my room without my knowing. I told her, in all honesty, that I was so busy helping the video editors work on the project that I hadn't noticed the students leaving. All the while, those video editors were working under a tight deadline and were beyond frustrated that they were doing all of the work for the project. Their parents were frustrated as well and did not hold back on their criticism throughout the rest of the project.

At this point, I wanted to pull the plug and move on to other subjects because clearly too much time was being wasted, but I couldn't. Our class had made a commitment to those veterans, and we couldn't just scrap what we were doing. As a result, the next several weeks were total mayhem. By the end of the project, the films were substandard at best. Because only one student worked on it the whole time, the quality went down the longer they had to slave over it. Many details were missed, because only one set of eyes saw the film before it was presented. The final presentation to the veterans felt like a disaster when the audio of several films didn't work, veteran names were misspelled, and some films weren't even ready to play at all, leaving attending veterans without a film to their name. On top of this, my students learned relatively little about World War II, my confidence in my first year of teaching was shot, and I swore I'd never do a group project again.

Like, ever.

But I did. Thanks to lots of trial and error and many, many tweaks along the way, I have completed that World War II project with my classes many times since that first year. (It turns out you forget your pain the further you get from it.) I now assign only two students to edit footage because I know that task requires a maximum of two people. Other tasks such as creating podcasts, creative writing, and artwork are assigned to other group members. I also use accountability systems and have project management techniques to schedule work time.

I have learned that collaboration wasn't the problem with that first World War II project; the problem was the fact that there wasn't any.

Teaching collaboration can be difficult, but it is not impossible.

I'll take that a step further: when you have the right tools and processes to facilitate group work with your students, collaboration can provide some of the most gratifying, memorable, and transformational learning students will ever experience. When kids work on meaningful tasks that require collaboration, what they can accomplish is boundless. It's especially effective when the collaborative task itself—and not just the teacher—requires that students contribute their varying skill sets, passions, and personalities to produce a specific result.

In a 2016 article for *Research Matters*, University of Cambridge researchers Simon Child and Stuart Shaw[3] wrote that learning is actually more effective when done collaboratively than when done individually. They argued that collaborative learning has advantages over individual problem solving because it fosters an effective division of labor and incorporates multiple sources of knowledge and perspectives as well as more creative group solutions. Collaboration, they continued, has also been found to increase students' social competencies and their abilities to help others and resolve conflicts.

I have seen this happen. When collaborating with others, students are no longer alone in processing information. They are sharing it and synthesizing it together. Problem solving is no longer limited to one brain but uses the intelligence and knowledge of a group.

Teaching collaboration is not only about preparing students for a future where they will need this skill. It's maximizing their learning in the present. Learning to collaborate will actually help students succeed as individuals. Successful individuals will contribute to the success of a group, both emotionally and academically. The opportunities for learning are richer when in groups. Complex and meaningful projects can be accomplished in groups. Learning how to care for other people's thoughts and opinions while representing your own happens in groups.

Collaboration can be a wonderful key to success.

It can only happen if we teach collaboration well and have tools and processes to make it effective. We must continually find new ways to inspire students to work together and realize what they can achieve when learning becomes about *us* rather than *me*.

That's what this book is all about.

CHAPTER 1

CREATING A COLLABORATIVE CULTURE

The cactus thrives in the desert while the fern thrives in the wetland. The fool will try to plant them in the same flower box.

—Vera Nazarian, *The Perpetual Calendar of Inspiration*

A huge oak tree in my front yard allows hardly any sun to hit the flower beds along my house. For almost every hour of the day, my front yard is covered in shade. When I first moved in, I went to a nursery to buy flowers and plants to adorn these beds in color. I found dahlias that burned like the sunset, their petals stretching wider than my hands. Zinnias that looked like you could squeeze them and cause paint to run onto the ground. Sunflowers that would make Van Gogh's mouth water. I couldn't wait to fill the hatchback of my Subaru with these flowers and plant them along the brick of my new home.

Then I noticed each of these had a tag that said, "Needs Full Sun." For a moment, I paused and wondered about that oak tree, but quickly dismissed the tag as more of a suggestion than a requirement. I loaded the car with as many plants and flowers as I could fit inside and planted them under that red oak.

A month later, they were all dead.

It turned out that "Needs Full Sun" was not a suggestion. The flowers I desperately wanted for my yard needed a certain environment to survive. They needed hours and hours of sun to grow, bloom, and grace my landscape beds with their wonder. I would have had to cut down the oak tree, and since I'd just spent a month's salary on flowers, that wasn't going to happen. Today my beds are filled with shade-tolerant, monochromatic hostas, and I'm green with envy of my neighbors' sunny yards.

Expecting a group of students—who have always approached learning from an individual perspective—to work together, have creative breakthroughs, and be more efficient than when working alone is like planting knockout roses in the shade. You've planted these amazing flowers but given them none of what they need to survive. Collaboration requires intentionality and a culture that allows it to thrive. Only when this culture exists and is continually nurtured can collaboration be successful and not something that will make you want to rip your hair out.

Many teachers want to do collaborative work and often start with a group project. The problem is that their students are used to an environment that operates on *individual* assignments, *individual* grades, and *individual* progress. Seating arrangements, assessments systems, classroom protocols, and even the nature of most classes are all designed for the enlightenment of the individual student. Most K–12 settings lack an environment that supports successful collaboration. As a result, these lone collaborative projects, which are like small islands in a vast ocean of individualism, usually fail, making it that much easier to write off group work and return to what is safer and easier.

Just because people are communal beings does not mean they naturally know how to be productive communally. They have to be taught what collaboration is and what it is not, what it looks like, and what purpose it will serve in their learning. That means teachers, from the start of every school year, must be intentional about creating a collaborative culture. They have to lay the foundation for a collaborative culture, always assuming that their students are not yet skilled collaborators. The work of establishing a collaborative culture with a new group of students requires three major components:

Clarity

Reflection

Intrinsic motivation

These components, which we will explore further, have to be introduced before anything else in a collaborative classroom. Building culture is about creating a place people want to be. This is why in my high school classrooms, the first week of the school year never covered any content work. I always spent the first weeks setting the tone for the rest of the year, building relationships with students, and helping them get to know each other so that they felt safe and comfortable working hard in that environment the rest of the year. There's obviously a time sacrifice involved in doing this, but establishing a collaborative culture is essential and sets your class up for success.

Establishing Clarity

Students need to have clarity when entering a collaborative classroom. Moving from an individual focus to a group focus can be jarring for many students. It's like plucking a fish out of the ocean and expecting it to breathe on land. Students should know from the first day how your class might be different from what they are used to and what your expectations are in a collaborative environment. If students are not introduced to a collaborative classroom with clarity, it will lead to friction and resistance down the line, which is a natural reaction.

I've worked with many schools to help their staffs navigate project-based learning (PBL) and innovate their teaching methods. In too many instances, an administrator brings me in to work with teachers to help them completely flip their learning models, with the expectation that everyone would teach using this new approach from then on. A few teachers in every group are excited about learning new processes, but everyone is obligated to be there. Most of the experienced teachers sit with their arms crossed, projecting that here-we-go-again attitude, and are clearly not thrilled to be learning another new model they don't believe will work.

I often get questions like, "Do we have to implement everything you are going to talk about today?" or "Is this going to become a part of our evaluations?" If the principal isn't in the room, someone might even ask, "Three years ago we adopted a different learning model. Do we really need to do this again?"

It's become apparent to me after doing the professional developments (PDs) for a while that I can't just dive into the content of my workshop. I cannot simply walk in and begin to teach and try to inspire teachers to push their boundaries and try this methodology I know to be effective and transformational. I have to first provide clarity and understanding if I ever hope to inspire others to try it out. Many teachers have worked in a certain type of environment for years, and they are most comfortable with what they know. Their resistance, I think, is rooted more in skepticism than arrogance. They have had so many new ideas thrown at them with little explanation that they now harbor a large degree of skepticism.

There has to be a foundation for innovation before that new learning can occur. This foundation often does not get laid, and the result is new systems failing and an inevitable return to the previous model.

The same is true for students. Whether you teach first graders or college seniors, most of your students have that bad taste in their mouths from when working with others has gone wrong. For many students, collaboration was not a positive experience, and so many will be hesitant about entering a collaborative classroom. Before diving into any collaborative work, give students a chance to call out reasons they do not like it.

Start by having them write their reasons, giving the prompt: "Make a list of reasons why group work is difficult."

Every single student should be able to generate a list. For even the most skilled collaborators, the work is difficult at times.

Once students have their lists, let them share their responses aloud and make sure not to minimize anything that they say. Listen to them; allow them to be honest as they slam collaboration, which they most likely will. I've encountered few students (and adults) who enjoyed collaborative work before they learned how to do it successfully. They need to know that you understand the struggle and are not naive about the challenges of collaboration.

You also hate when one person does all the work and everyone else gets credit. You get why they'd be hesitant to work with people they don't like. Make clear that you understand their resistance and that those are issues you will work on during the school year. (By the way, this is exactly what I do with participants in my workshops.)

Class Contract Gallery Walk

Once grievances have been aired, shift the conversation to what you can do to make the bad parts of collaboration happen less and less. "What are some things our class can do to make sure we don't hate, but actually enjoy, working with each other?"

This conversation is a great way to introduce the idea of creating a class contract. A class contract, also known as a social contract, is a list of norms and expectations for a class that students help create and then abide by the rest of the year. In a collaborative classroom, everything on the contract should be aimed at improving the way students work together. Start by asking a handful of key questions and having students write their responses. A fun way to do this is to set up a gallery walk, with the questions written on posters, and have students write their responses on sticky notes and place them on the posters throughout the room. As students silently walk around to each poster, if they see a sticky note with something they agree with, they should put a check mark next to it.

Here are some examples of helpful focus questions:

- What does a productive class look like?
- How do you want to be treated in here?
- What does a healthy class discussion look like?
- What does it mean to have a safe classroom—physically and emotionally?

- What actions show someone is being responsible?
- What does it look like to be involved in your learning?
- What does it look like to be involved in each other's learning?

After students respond and place their sticky notes around the room, have them divide into small groups and discuss their answers. The next step is to take the discussion to the whole group and talk about everything students wrote down. What responses have the most check marks? What do they value most in a classroom environment? Synthesize their responses down to a few essential rules and norms everyone can agree to, print these norms on a poster, and hang them in a visible location in your classroom. This poster can be student-designed and be visually attractive or it can be as plain as print on paper. What's most important is that it was created by the entire class and remains on display for your class every day. You can even have students sign the bottom of it as proof that they have all agreed to abide by their own rules.

A finished class contract could look something like this:

- I will listen to others, whether I agree with them or not.
- I will let others know if they have hurt or offended me.
- I will work hard to succeed but also to help others succeed.
- I will always strive to meet deadlines.
- I will always strive to do my best work.
- I will take risks and challenge myself and others.

This contract can be used for accountability and as a reminder to students of what they agreed to at the beginning of the year. More importantly, creating a class contract is a way to provide clarity to students about the expectations for your collaborative classroom. They will learn early on that there are specific traits—particularly respect for one another—that are valued in your classroom. This clarity will help pave the way for healthy collaboration the rest of the year.

Practicing Reflection

Part of growing in any skill or ability is giving yourself time to reflect so you can make iterations and improve. Life is too busy and too noisy to make meaningful adjustments on the fly. We have to develop a habit to pause and reflect regularly. In our personal lives, this can mean journaling, honest discussions with loved ones, or even just turning off the radio or podcast on the way to work and driving in silence. It's in this intentional time that we can discover why certain class activities didn't work, how to mend a relationship with a coworker, what we need to cut to find balance in life, or other challenges that need to be reflected on to be solved.

This same intentional space needs to be given to students if we want them to grow as collaborators and possess lasting skills beyond our classrooms. Reflection needs to become a regular process in the collaborative culture.

A great way to begin this reflection habit with students is to have them practice it at the beginning of the year. In the first week of the school year, as your students are getting to know you, each other, and your class, have them complete a highly collaborative task and reflect on the task afterwards. Whichever task they do, make sure the reflection that follows highlights the need for collaboration during the task.

The Missing Tape Project

In this collaborative activity, students work in small groups of three or four with the challenge of building the strongest platform using nothing more than thirty popsicle sticks, two feet of yarn, and one foot of Scotch tape. After giving each group their materials, tell them that they have ten minutes to build the strongest platform, which needs to be at least three inches tall, and after ten minutes you will see whose platform can support the most weight.

Pretty simple, right?

Right before you start the timer and students begin building, announce that there is one more rule: no talking.

If students say any words, their tower will be destroyed and they will have to start all over, but the timer does not reset.

Start the timer and allow building to begin. After about two minutes, make an announcement to the class that you need to speak to one member from each group outside of your classroom, and ask them to bring the group's strip of tape. Once all of those students, who have their group's tape are outside of your class, tell them you will be right back and close the door. For the rest of the time left on the clock, leave that group outside. Everyone still building will, of course, get frustrated and want their tape back but won't be able to complain out loud, and the timer will still be going, so they are going to have to improvise. Meanwhile, the students outside of the classroom will inevitably start banging on the door to get in, and you can just give them a nice sinister smile but no explanation.

When there are thirty seconds left on the timer, let the students with the tape back in. They most likely will run to their groups, but there will not be enough time left to make a difference. When the timer goes off, expect to hear a barrage of complaints about how you rigged the system. I find it best to just ignore them and walk around with the weights to test out their platforms. Almost every time I have ever done this activity, the platforms are completely ineffective. It's near impossible to build a strong three-inch tower with only popsicle sticks and yarn in ten minutes without saying a word.

After the failed tests of the platforms, tell students you are giving them ten more minutes to build their platforms, only this time they can talk, and you promise not to take away their tape. After sitting silently for ten minutes, students relish being allowed to talk this time, and the classroom will get loud as they discuss how to build the strongest tower.

Test them again with the weights, and you'll find that most groups built a successful tower.

This is a really fun activity and an ice breaker that requires collaboration, creativity, communication, and critical thinking. It's also great because you get a chance to kindly torture your students in that first round, which is always a bonus.

The real strength of this activity, however, comes from the reflection that follows. Have students first turn and talk to each other about why the second round of building was so much more successful than the first round, and then have them share with the class.

The obvious responses will be "Because you took our tape!" and "Because we weren't allowed to talk," and maybe even, "Because I barely whispered, and you smashed our tower!" (I'm telling you—this activity makes me a little evil.)

Then have students discuss what they did well during the second round. Following this discussion, ask what lessons can be learned from this activity.

"Don't trust our teacher!"

All right, now that we've gotten that out of the system, what other lessons did we learn?

"If you have an idea, you need to speak up."

"If someone has something the rest of the group needs, they need to be at school."

"When someone in the group is not present, it's hard to get work done."

"For group work to be successful, everyone needs to be a part of it."

This activity introduces a few of the truths that students will continue to discover throughout the year in a collaborative classroom. And when needed, you can always reference the tower-building activity and the discussion the class had about how essential communication and collaboration are to success. One time after this activity, a student made a poster for my classroom that said, "Don't Be the Missing Tape." It became our class mantra, and students said that phrase to each other if someone was not pulling their weight during a collaborative activity.

The power of this exercise lies in the work students did but also in the reflection that followed. That is when important lessons were verbalized and began to sink in. Reflection is something students will constantly be doing as they assess themselves and others (see Chapter 5) and process successes and failures. It must be introduced early for students to learn its value and grow used to a practice that they will observe regularly throughout the year (and hopefully, life).

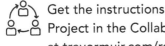 Get the instructions for The Missing Tape Project in the Collaborative Classroom Toolkit at trevormuir.com/resources.

Building Intrinsic Motivation

The final step in laying the foundation for a collaborative culture is making sure students understand why it is so necessary. They need to know why they are going to be stretched in ways they haven't been stretched before. It's important for them to learn why they will be put in groups when most of school for them has been done individually—and when it was in groups, they didn't enjoy it. Students need to be informed of the creative power of collaboration if we are to expect them to embrace it in our classes.

In an ideal world, you could inform students by telling them about the need to collaborate. You could cite the facts I stated in the Introduction about the workforce demanding it of them. You could share an anecdote of collaboration gone wrong in your own life and how you wished you would have been taught to collaborate when you were in school. You could give an inspirational speech about what happens when we combine creative energy and use our collective minds to solve problems and create new things. And then thank them for coming to your TED Talk.

Let me save you the headache. I've tried this, and I was met with many eye rolls as students thought, "Yeah, whatever. I've done enough group projects to know that you are full of it."

Students have to discover the value of collaboration themselves and realize the intrinsic motivation of collaborative work rather than be told about it. It's this intrinsic motivation that will get the most out of students when collaborating. When collaborative work is at its full potential and there is a synergy among group members that does not exist when working individually, it is truly a sight to behold. It's like a soccer team that works as one organism and can seem to do no wrong. Or a symphony that is so in sync the audience forgets it has individual members. This is what collaboration can be at its finest in the classroom, and students need to know early on that this joy is attainable and worth striving for.

In an interview with the website *Fast Company,* Justin Rosenstein, one of the founders of the tech company Asana, which was named by *Entrepreneur Magazine* as one of the top workplace cultures in America, ascribes their success to a work environment rooted in collaboration.[1] At the heart of his company is the belief that employees should "work hard, live well." Rosenstein notes that "Treating each other well, being respectful to each other, building a culture you actually want to live in, these are all things that make people happier, and in the end, more productive."

A culture that makes work enjoyable will produce better work. At the beginning of the year, it's important to introduce to students the concept that collaboration is something they can love, not simply survive. We must show them that collaboration can be satisfying, make their work better, and add its own intrinsic value to their lives.

I have found it helpful to give students an early opportunity to win at a collaborative task. They have to see what they are capable of when working together, especially when the task requires it. In that first culture-building week, devise an activity that allows this to happen.

Here are a few tips to keep in mind:

Strive for Authenticity

Many of the best lessons come from experiences that feel authentic and even spontaneous. As the planner of these experiences, you can know what you want students to get out of them and design them accordingly, but the less forced they feel, the better students will respond. No one wants to feel like a character on *The Office*, forced by a goofy boss to sit through ridiculous team-building activities. Bosses like Michael Scott aren't nearly as endearing in real life.

Collaborative opportunities abound if you take the time to brainstorm. Plan a collaborative competition. Organize a scavenger hunt. Play a sport like ultimate frisbee. See if your school will fund a day on a ropes course. Have your students create some silly videos. Do a storytelling activity. The key is to craft an activity that won't make your students feel as if you are forcing a lesson down their throats.

Require Interdependence

It's always helpful to ask this question at the outset: *Can the activity be done better if students work alone?* If the answer is yes, pick something different. You want your collaborative activity to be something that requires students to work together. It's under these circumstances that students will become aware that sometimes the best work happens in groups. Make sure the activity's success requires students to communicate with each other. It also should be clear that the outcome will fail or at leas,ooms. We want the students in our collaborative classrooms to have fun and embrace the idea of working with others. Kids should be smiling during the activity and after they finish. I've had students play tug of war over a mud pit and had a competition to see who can build a fire the fastest with only one match (I obviously had outdoor space for these two). I've let my students create music videos introducing themselves to the class and had them design board games to be played by elementary students at the end of the week. All of these activities were fun. They required effort, but the students had a blast in the process. This initial introduction to collaboration sets the stage for work that was usually more toned down, but equally embraced.

At the start of one school year, my principal had the entire staff meet in a conference room, and we all expected a traditional back-to-school PD where we'd sit for hours, maybe do some ice breakers, and wish we had time to set up our classrooms. But the principal gave everyone a gift card for a go-kart and laser tag place. For the next three hours, sixty high school teachers did nothing but smash into each other in go-karts, battle each other in laser tag, and sit around tables and stuff ourselves with all-you-can-eat pizza. That was our PD day.

It was the most memorable and effective PD day I can remember. I got to know my colleagues on a new level. We worked together outside of our profession so that when we returned to the work of teaching, we could collaborate like never before. Some people thought my principal was silly and even wasteful for spending almost two thousand dollars for his teachers to ride go-karts together. The expense, however, was well worth it because those same teachers were later able to sit down together and work through student issues, plan engaging curriculum, brainstorm how to improve school culture, and realize they were not alone in the hard work of being an educator. I saw it as a wise investment in building a collaborative culture.

Setting Up Your Culture for Success

We have to view the laying of the foundation for a collaborative culture in our classrooms as an investment. Students can't be expected to seamlessly transfer into an environment where they must rely on and work with others to succeed. They have to be introduced to this new ecosystem with intention and guided into it with activities that show them that collaboration is worth the effort. We can show them that collaboration does not have to be like the failed group projects of their pasts.

This lesson might not set in the first week of the school year after a few team-building activities and discussions about collaboration. It will likely take them getting their hands dirty and achieving real results from collaborative work. Successful collaboration cannot happen if we don't first lay a foundation for a collaborative culture. "Needs Full Sun" is not a suggestion.

Reflection

1. What are some of the largest hurdles in establishing a collaborative culture in your school and classroom?
2. Create your own list of reasons for why group work is difficult.
3. Think of an instance as a student when you experienced some of these collaboration struggles.
4. Now think of an instance as a professional when you have struggled with or experienced negative collaboration.

Take Action

Throughout the rest of the book, keep this list on hand and seek ways to set up a collaborative culture in which these struggles can be eased or avoided for your students.

#CollaborativeClassroom

CHAPTER 2

TEACHING STUDENTS TO RELY ON THEMSELVES AND OTHERS

The challenge of every team is to build a feeling of oneness, of dependence on one another because the question is usually not how well each person performs, but how well they work together.

—Vince Lombardi, head coach of the Green Bay Packers

Billionaire Elon Musk[1] believes human extinction on earth is inevitable, and he has spent his fortune from starting the companies PayPal and Tesla to create a rocket company, with the aim of colonizing the planet Mars and creating a second Earth for humans to live and thrive on.

What are you doing with your life?

When Musk first started SpaceX, there was a notion that the company was not feasible and could not achieve success. Loren Thompson[2] wrote in a *Forbes Magazine* article that "SpaceX could find themselves in decaying orbits in the years ahead." Private space travel is too expensive. The task is too large. There are too many moving pieces to possibly build a rocket capable of not only leaving Earth's orbit but entering the orbit of another planet within this lifetime. Astrophysicist Neil DeGrasse Tyson, in 2015, told *The Verge* magazine, "The delusion is thinking that SpaceX is going to lead the space frontier."[3]

Three years later, SpaceX launched the Falcon Heavy Rocket, the most powerful rocket in the world, into outer space, setting the stage for a planned unmanned mission to Mars in 2022 and a manned mission two years later. If you're reading this book after 2025, you'll know whether SpaceX stuck to their schedule. Feel free to hop in a time machine and let us know. (Also, thanks for buying this book. Hopefully schools are collaborating more by now.)

The fact is, SpaceX is meeting these goals despite the scope of the task. Part of its success is *because* of the scope and size of the company's aspirations. SpaceX's mission statement is "Enabling people to live on other planets." That is the motivation for all other work, which at times can look disconnected from the overall task. Devising reusable rockets or launching satellites into space for the U.S. government is not directly Mars-related, but it's funding the projects that will take humans to Mars. Musk, the CEO and leader of the company, is constantly stressing this point to employees and uses it to inspire all of their work. This sense of purpose is at the heart of the company and is why its seven thousand employees are achieving such astounding accomplishments.

A huge factor in the SpaceX team's ability to successfully combine their talents and skills to accomplish tremendous endeavors is their motivation. Musk's management style is defined by inspiring employees and helping them know why they are doing the work they are doing.

One of the most vexing issues teachers have with group work is keeping students on task. On the surface, a collaborative classroom might seem to require less work for teachers than a traditional classroom. The teacher is not standing at the front of the room delivering long lectures. They are not gathering all of the information students need and delivering it to them. Students are doing the work of obtaining the knowledge they need, working with each other, and leaving the teacher to observe.

Wrong! That's not how it works. Teachers often face an increased workload when their students collaborate. Whether putting out fires from group conflicts, struggling to keep students on task, or making sure the right content and skills are being learned and developed, managing collaborative time can be extremely difficult.

I conducted a survey of more than five hundred teachers, attempting to learn what teachers struggle most with when it comes to assigning group work. The results were not too surprising. Given the options of "assessing collaboration," "time management," "creating groups," "team accountability," and "constant off-task behavior," off-task behavior had nearly double the number of responses of all the other options. Managing students and their time is clearly a shared struggle.

How do we foster a collaborative environment where students learn interdependence, relying on each other to complete tasks, as well as independence and managing their time, resources, challenges, and thinking without constant help from their teacher? How can the class be successful without the teacher doing all the work?

Cast a Vision for Meaningful Work

Effective project management starts with student ownership. Like employees at SpaceX, when students know why they are doing the work they are doing, and the work actually matters to them, containing deep intrinsic and extrinsic motivation, they will work harder and smarter to complete tasks. The work has to matter to students for them to own it.

This is why I'm such a fan of project-based learning (PBL). At its core, PBL is about giving authenticity to the work students do. They are still learning content and becoming more proficient in all of the subjects that school traditionally requires, and with PBL, that learning is tied to solving meaningful problems. Project-based learning isn't the same as doing projects. Projects, in the traditional sense, often mean creating something at the end of the learning unit. A class reads a book and then creates a diorama. Or students learn about volcanoes and then make a model of one. These types of projects are not required for the learning to happen but are more like assessments of the learning.

Project-based learning, however, is about learning that is dependent on the project. Students learn by doing and solving and failing and toiling. It's more hands-on and memorable, like a great story. The authenticity of the project, the need to solve a real problem with real consequences, is what drives the learning. When students engage in this type of work, it provides them with the type of motivation that makes them want to take ownership.

Let's say students in a science class find out that an invasive plant species is taking over a local public park they frequently visit. This might bother them, especially if the students discover that there is something that can be done about it. They do some research and decided to organize a community event where neighbors come out and compete to see who can pull up the most of this invasive species from the park. To get community members to come to the event, students will have to educate them about the problem by creating flyers, making public service announcement (PSA) videos, and speaking to the local media. To educate the community, the students will first have to educate themselves.

At this point, students are learning about invasive species and the impact they can have, not because their teacher said so or for a specific letter grade, they are learning this science content to improve their community. There is a deeper motivation for excellent work. When they are in the midst of the work and all the stressors that go with collaboration, they will know there is a greater purpose behind it. To solve the problem in front of them, they have to work together.

Students will take ownership of their work and value it more when that work matters to them. This is a crucial component in students having autonomy. Strong student engagement most often leads to a well-managed classroom. Perhaps the best classroom management strategy is finding ways to make learning authentic. Students work harder when the work matters. They make sure their peers and group mates work harder as well. If an authentic deadline is approaching, such as the invasive species community event, students will rise to that occasion.

I've seen so often when students are not rising and are not contributing, those students are held accountable by their peers out of necessity. When students are invested, failure is not an option, and this promotes interdependence. Students are forced to rely on each other because otherwise the project will not succeed, and the problem will not be solved.

Set Clear Goals

Self-managed groups require clear goals. Students need to know what they are working toward, as well as what is expected of them, if we want them to achieve success. At the start of any collaborative work, whether it's a project, individual task, or discussion, have students first discuss precisely what they are trying to accomplish. After their discussion, each group member should write this goal down; if you choose to, have them submit it to you. You can do a quick review of their responses and make sure everyone is clear about their tasks and where they are headed. This ensures that every student was at least made aware of what they needed to do at the beginning of the work.

Too many times, I thought I was clear with students about what their tasks were, only to find out at the end of class or even the end of a several-week project that they were not clear at all. Providing this clarity from the outset can eliminate this problem, as well as eliminate the time wasted from having to restate the task again when the rest of the class already moved on.

A great place to have students write the project goal is on the Group Contract, which we talk about in Chapter 3.

Create Structure

I'm the type of person who flies at thirty thousand feet, a big-picture thinker. Precision has never been my strong suit, and so I have always struggled with this. I'm not sure if organizational skills can be attributed to nature or nurture, but I definitely do not feel like they are something I was born with. This is why my greatest struggles leading a collaborative classroom arise from lacking these skills. Whenever I have tried to wing it and slack on providing structure for students to work in, the work suffers.

This is because students need structure. A child's brain development relies on guidance and routines. Harvard psychologist Karen Postal, PhD, explains in *Psychology Today* how our executive functions, our decision-making abilities, develop throughout childhood and adolescence. Structure and guidance from adults essentially provide that function of the brain for students as they are developing it themselves. Dr. Postal writes that "structures can assist a child's brain to learn more efficiently, as if they possessed a more mature frontal system." Choice and autonomy are still beneficial, but they should happen within a well-organized structure.

When I assumed that students would just figure out who was going to do what in their groups and left them to their own devices to do it, often they were left floundering at their desks, which led to me hovering over them and managing their groups—exactly what we don't want. Here are some ways to provide structure in a collaborative classroom:

Assign Roles

One of the best ways to provide structure but still empower students in collaborative work is to assign students roles within their groups. Roles provide specificity to the work each individual does. When students have different jobs and responsibilities within a group, they're less likely to feel left out and disengaged, and more likely to stay on task. Each role comes with certain expectations, and again, students (and the rest of us) do better when they know what is expected of them.

Different tasks require different roles. If students are engaging in brainstorming, it's essential to have someone leading the process (the leader), someone to clarify thoughts and ideas (the clarifier), and someone to record them (the recorder). For project work, it's helpful to have roles such as leader, researcher, presenter, technology specialist, and timekeeper. And specific tasks require specific roles, so a video project might have an editor, script supervisor, researcher, and music-finder.

These give students direction and responsibility. It's also beneficial to alternate roles regularly so that students are exposed to new tasks and responsibilities. Students will excel more in areas they are more comfortable in and be stretched and challenged in unfamiliar roles. This is exactly why roles are so important. They teach students new skills and reinforce old ones. When a student is made the leader of a discussion, they are gaining valuable experience in leadership. If they are assigned as clarifier, they are forced to listen and process information in a way they may never have before. Their success in their roles becomes the team's success. The task or project cannot achieve excellence without every one of the roles contributing. Students learn to rely on each other and develop true interdependence.

Use a Project Management Log

Project Management Log

Task (Next Steps)	Who Is Responsible	Role	Due Date	Status

Get the PML Template in the Collaborative Classroom
Toolkit at trevormuir.com/resources.

The Project Management Log (PML) is a task list that students reference every day at the outset of project work time. As a group, students discuss what needs to be worked on during that specific session and write down who is doing what. The PML also records everyone's roles and tasks, ensuring everyone has a task to complete. As a result, everyone has clarity on what they need to do and when they need to do it by.

The PML gets rid of the free-for-all mentality, what I used to have when telling students to do whatever they needed to get done, without any structure. Now, their time is guided by the tasks on the PML. Students can learn to use this as a tool to manage their own time, but also to hold their teammates accountable. If someone is off task, a teammate can ask them, "Did you complete this specific task that you said you would?" If the answer is no, they can kindly ask them to get back to work. If the answer is yes, they can help them figure out other tasks to work on for the group (more on this in Chapter 3).

The PML is also a great tool for teachers to use to monitor the progress of each group. I often ask students to show me their PMLs before they start collaborative work time. It lets me know whether students have a plan for the day or whether I need to help them develop one. It also can be used as an exit slip at the end of each class; ask students to fill out the status of their task or create their task list for the following day. The PML serves as a formative assessment to gauge which groups need extra help and which are on track.

The PML helps students learn to divide and conquer, and if used as a vital tool, ensures that tasks are completed and deadlines are met.

Tech hint: A great, free, online tool your class can use as a PML is trello.com. It is incredibly easy to use, and students can organize their daily tasks in shared groups on this site. Using a PML doc is great, but Trello definitely has some add-ons that are useful.

Have Checkpoints and Deadlines

Collaborative work must have tight checkpoints and deadlines. Strict deadlines apply pressure that unlimited time does not. When students know their time is finite and that the success of their work requires meeting these deadlines, they will be more diligent. This is especially true if the deadlines are authentic.

If students have to complete a project on time because the teacher says so or because there will be a penalty to their grade if they do not, many students will respond positively. This has been the primary motivator used in schools for over a century, and students are conditioned to that. However, many students could not care less about their grade and would rather spend group work time chatting and relaxing rather than meeting a deadline.

It's these students who often make us want to pull out whatever hair we have left and swear never to attempt group work again. This is why we need better motivators. If students are creating presentations on pollution that will be delivered to the mayor or are making comic books that will be read to kids at a children's hospital, not completing the project on time is unacceptable. These are not due dates that can just be pushed back, and late work will not just be given a late grade. These are authentic deadlines that carry natural consequences if they are not met.

At the start of a collaborative project, provide students with a project calendar containing the specific dates certain items need to be completed. Impress on them why it's important for these dates to be met, and discuss the consequences if they are not. If it's a smaller task, such as small group discussions, use a visual timer to provide this structure. When a timer is counting down in front of them and is strictly used to manage time, students will quickly learn that there is not time to goof around at the beginning of an activity. Give students a structure for their work time, highlighting why it's important to stick to this schedule.

Teach Creative Problem Solving

Our ability to solve problems and think critically is easy to take for granted. As educators, we experience countless problems on a daily basis. From Wi-Fi going down at the start of a lesson, to instructional videos not loading, to having half the class be absent on the day you were planning to introduce an important new topic, to the myriad of other obstacles that force us to solve and then adjust on the fly, teaching is loaded with problem solving. It's when you were faced with these problems that you were forced to figure out how to deal with them. Your critical thinking abilities are not completely innate, but were developed from experience, like that time your lesson plan bombed and you had to figure out how to teach a different way on the spot.

This is why students can be needy at times when given autonomy in collaborative groups. When they hit roadblocks, they don't know how to get over them. When they come from an education system that primarily gives them the information rather than helping them to find it themselves, can we really blame them? Teachers have to be intentional about teaching their students how to solve problems.

The Creative Problem-Solving Method

One way to teach problem solving is to practice it within a specific framework. Once students become comfortable using the framework to identify and overcome issues, they can use its principles in a more informal way whenever necessary. However, as we are instilling in students possibly the most useful skill they will ever obtain in school, it's important to be explicit with a problem-solving structure.

The Creative Problem Solving (CPS) framework is one of the most simple but useful methods to teach students to solve problems. The framework looks like this:

1. Clarify the problem.
2. Generate ideas to solve it.
3. Evaluate the ideas for the best solutions.
4. Plan how to solve it.

Whether your students are solving an algebra problem or trying to figure out how to use video editing software, the CPS framework can be used to keep them moving forward. We want to embed this process into our students' brains, making it a method that they go to any time they encounter issues. To do so, it should be modeled to them before being put into practice.

To teach and model CPS, start with a broad scenario that needs the method to solve it. After modeling with a broad subject, students can begin to use it for more realistic problems. Naming the steps of the method to your students, give them an age-appropriate scenario, like the story of an oil spill in the ocean and the permanent impact on the environment it could have if not cleaned up.

You have stated the problem; now ask students to clarify it. They should gather and restate all of the data you presented, clearly stating the challenge and setting an objective they wish to meet. Emphasize that it is difficult to solve a problem if you are not perfectly clear about what the problem is. As a class, devise a challenge question that needs to be solved, such as *How can we clean up the oil spill?*

Give students time to research and talk with each other about potential solutions to the problem. Any possible answer to the challenge question should be suggested and written down. When generating ideas, it's essential that students do not judge ideas or limit the ideas that are suggested. In the next step, students will have time to scrutinize and judge; this step is about getting many ideas out there from everyone in the group.

After you have a list of ideas, the class can evaluate them to decide which is best, how they can be combined, how to strengthen them, and which to discard. This should be a discussion, and students should be vocal about their thoughts. Encourage them to be open to each other's ideas and start sentences with "I like" and "I wonder."

"*I like* the idea of using a giant sponge to clean up the oil."

"*I wonder* how we can get a giant sponge out to the ocean."

Remind students that during this stage of the process, ideas are being judged, not people. Keep the language impersonal, and be honest while striving to find the best solution to the problem. After an idea is selected, students can plan how to implement it. This is where roles and tasks are assigned. Students believe they now have an answer to their challenge question and are making a plan to act.

Once students understand the CPS framework, encourage them to use it whenever they encounter an obstacle. If used well, the teacher will see that their assistance is required much less during collaborative time.

I used to give students a task, such as creating a poster, and required that it be done digitally. They would have a clear idea of what I wanted them to do, but five minutes later, I would get called to every single group by students asking me what graphic design tool they should use, and then inevitably, how to use it. Too much time was spent showing students how to do the work instead of me listening in and seeing what they were doing.

When students are taught how to solve problems, instead of calling me over, they figure it out themselves. They clarify the problem—how to create a poster—and generate all the ideas needed to create it. They use Photoshop, Canva.com, Google Docs, and other tools they discover during this stage of the process and have a conversation evaluating their ideas.

The more students solve problems this way, the larger variety of problems they will solve with it. From group conflict to not knowing how to find a piece of information when writing a paper, students will learn to become more interdependent and independent. These are the traits our students possibly need most in the evolving world. Our society needs problem solvers. We don't need information-regurgitators who can just follow instructions and memorize. We need people who aren't afraid of challenges, who don't shy away from problems but see them as something they can and will overcome together.

A process such as this takes time. Many students have been hand-fed their learning in school and at home, and having to solve problems independently without the constant guidance of a teacher is new to them. Have patience as they develop these traits. Understand that just because you are a problem-solving wizard (because what teacher isn't?) doesn't mean they are. A collaborative classroom is sometimes a more challenging classroom, especially in its early stages. It's tempting to be a "lawnmower teacher," mowing down any obstacles our students face and solving their problems for them. If we want our students to develop these skills, we must have patience and be willing to let them struggle. Luckily, the product of our patience and their struggle is more independent yet communal people, something our society desperately needs more of, especially if it means getting to Mars someday.

Reflection

1. When has interdependence served you well in your own career?
2. Recall a time when you saw purpose and meaningful work increase student engagement.
3. What are some of your biggest reservations when it comes to student ownership and autonomy?
4. What are some activities you already assign in which your students could use Creative Problem Solving?

Take Action

Download the Project Management Log and design a task in which students can use it to organize and manage their time.

#CollaborativeClassroom

CHAPTER 3

HOW TO HOLD OTHERS ACCOUNTABLE

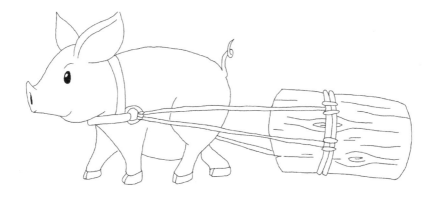

Responsibility equals accountability equals ownership. And a sense of ownership is the most powerful weapon a team or organization can have.

—Pat Summitt, eight-time NCAA National Championship winning basketball coach

One of the wisest literary characters ever written once said, "There are all kinds of courage. It takes a great deal of bravery to stand up to our enemies, but just as much to stand up to our friends. I therefore award ten points to Mr. Neville Longbottom."[1]

Harry Potter fans, you're welcome.

Professor Dumbledore awarded Neville those points because he took the unpopular action of holding his friends accountable. They were breaking the rules, despite the fact that their actions would affect everyone else, and he stood up to them. Although it was difficult, Neville made the right decision, and it paid off in the end.

One of the most difficult aspects of collaboration, one that lasts long into adulthood, is teammate accountability. When in the midst of a group project, many of us struggle to hold others accountable for fear of disrupting harmony. Evolutionary biologist David Barash argues in a *New York Times* article[2] that people are hard-wired for peacemaking. Citing examples throughout human history, Barash makes the case that the success of the human race can be attributed to our ability to avoid conflict and resolve differences. People are communal and desire relationships and acceptance, trying to avoid conflict at all costs. Essentially, those who avoid violent conflict are the ones who survive and continue the human race.

However, Barash says, the traits humans possess and use to avoid conflict are "communication, reconciliation, and cooperative problem solving."[2] Avoiding conflict does not mean one does not participate in it; it means they make every effort to keep it from escalating.

Being agreeable and not speaking truth to an issue is a short-term fix. It helps us to avoid hurting someone's feelings while also not feeling uncomfortable ourselves. Most people seek peace, and overall, an innate desire to seek peace is a good thing.

Peace is certainly important, but avoiding conflict can often be to our detriment. Delaying temporary discomfort over and over inevitably leads to serious issues later on.

I can't even count the number of times students have come to me at the end of a group project complaining that they had to do all the work and everyone else in the group slacked. I always respond by asking, "What did you do to hold them accountable?"

Usually, the answer is, "Nothing. I didn't want them to be mad at me."

I have to empathize with this point. We don't want to sow discord, especially with friends and the people we are close to, and this can lead to being exploited or taken advantage of.

I once worked on a team of teachers with the task to innovate the English curriculum. Everyone on the team agreed to this objective and committed to see it through. When we'd meet, however, one teacher was always on his laptop grading papers or even scrolling through Facebook. He never contributed to the conversation or offered to research a question someone might have. And the results showed. His class was stuck in another time period, and our department team never really achieved our whole vision because there wasn't complete buy-in. We wanted to change school culture, but that wasn't possible when a large portion of students in our school were in a class that was stuck in the past.

As a teacher who was passionate about finding new ways to engage students and building an English department known for incredible learning experiences, this was incredibly frustrating. As a team, we decided to make these changes, but they couldn't happen without everyone being on board. And this guy would not get on board.

I remember complaining to my wife, talking to other co-workers about it, venting to my principal, and even blogging about the situation.

But guess who I didn't talk to about my frustration?

You got it. I never once talked to this other teacher about the frustrations the group was having with him. The truth is, he was a really nice guy, and we always had a great time talking about football or our families. I didn't want to hurt his feelings, and I didn't want to feel uncomfortable bringing up the issues.

I avoided the temporary discomfort. As a result, the conflict was never solved. Our team achieved some success, but it never attained its full potential. Our mission *required* collaboration, and it wasn't fully getting it.

There's a chance this teacher had no idea people were not happy with his lack of involvement. He might have assumed that no news is good news. He also could have had reservations about the new protocols and the mission we were all on, and just did not voice them. I tend to be loud and outspoken, and it's entirely possible he felt unheard and so did not speak.

It's also possible he was just being lazy.

We never found out why because we didn't hold him accountable. And so someone could have said to me exactly what I now say to students when they complain about a slacker but did nothing to hold them accountable: "Sorry, but collaboration isn't just about doing your part. It's ensuring others do theirs."

This isn't necessarily fair, and that's often the response I get from students. "Why is it my job to make sure someone else is doing their work?"

It might not be your job in a traditional school system that is focused solely on the individual, but being on a team requires accountability. The ability to communicate and make sure everyone is contributing is essential to collaboration. I learned this the hard way—in college when those three pretty girls walked all over me and years later when my fellow teacher refused to participate—but it doesn't have to happen this way.

Hogs and Logs

One of the goals of a collaborative classroom is to minimize the impact of hogs and logs. The hogs are those students who insist on monopolizing all of the work. They are the ones who take over the bulk of an assignment or project, not allowing other group members to participate. Hogs exist for a number of reasons. The most prominent is that the hogs do not trust their group mates. School has made them so adept at succeeding individually that the risk of trusting others with their success is too great. To the hogs, relinquishing control can mean a risk of failure, and in their experience with school, failure is not an option.

Therefore, they hog the work, forcing themselves to sacrifice more time and energy than others, but also getting creative control, thereby not allowing others to contribute.

Now, I really don't believe students are born hogs. I think the system has created this trait, as well as the experience of working with logs: those students who are immobile, sluggish, and stagnant, who do nothing to contribute. Whether caused by laziness, apathy, or their own distrust, some students just do not put in the same effort as everyone else. This forces others to carry their slack. Ask any group of people why they do not like group projects, and the overwhelming response will be because of the logs. The injustice of someone riding on your coattail, doing nothing and yet reaping the benefits, is maddening.

Whether it's dead weight or a student who insists on taking over the entire workload, hogs and logs can be a recipe for disastrous collaboration. Luckily, tools and processes can help students no longer be hogs and logs.

Tools for Accountability

Holding someone accountable does not have to be a difficult task if you have some helpful tools, specific processes, and reasonable protocols in place. Here are a few that every classroom can use to practice accountability on the path to successful collaboration:

Group Contract

Group Contract

Team Members

Name	Email / Contact Info	Strengths / Areas for Growth	Role (This will be filled in once you have a better idea of the project)

I.   Project Goals *What is the goal of this project?*

II. Team Agreements

III. Accountability

List the process that your team will go through in order to hold each other accountable for the above agreements. Please note that if your team decides that members may be removed from the group, you must be able to demonstrate that the team has taken appropriate steps to intervene (such as documented warnings, meeting to discuss concerns, notify the teacher of concerns, etc)

IV. Team Signatures:

Name:	Signature:

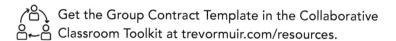 Get the Group Contract Template in the Collaborative Classroom Toolkit at trevormuir.com/resources.

At the beginning of any collaborative project, before any work takes place, students should fill out a group contract. A group contract is a shared document that the group members write together and sign. It's essentially a mutual agreement made by all group members to set the norms for collaboration throughout the project. This is a living document that can be referred to and used as a tool whenever necessary to help students hold each other accountable.

The creation of a group contract starts with a discussion among group members about each other's strengths and weaknesses concerning whatever project or task they are working on. If students are doing some type of art project, it's beneficial for everyone to know whether someone loves making art. If there is a video component, this is an opportunity for a student with video skills to let everyone else know. If the project involves public speaking and a student is deathly afraid of it, they would share this with their group members during this part of the process.

This does not mean that if someone is strong in a certain area they will be assigned a certain role or that a kid afraid of public speaking won't have to present. The point of this process is for students to get acquainted with one another, so they have extra knowledge to strengthen collaboration later on. Classroom relationships tend to be surface level, and what students know about each other is based on certain narrow information. When students are given a formal, directed time to talk with each other about personal strengths and room for growth, relationships go deeper. And I cannot say this enough: the heart of strong collaboration is found in relationships.

Within the context of the group contract, students must discuss what they expect from each other throughout the group project. A teacher can model or lead this discussion the first time, talking about what kind of agreements should be included in the contract. It might include team agreements such as these:

I will complete any task assigned to me by the group.

If I am sick or absent for some reason, I will check in with the group.

I will not use my headphones unless I am working on an individual task.

I will meet all deadlines that the group sets.

I will be open to constructive criticism from other group members.

It might be helpful to ask students, "What kind of things have bothered you before during group projects?" or "If you are on a team, what do you value most from your teammates?"

After gathering responses, let students know that the group contract is designed to help prevent these issues. Once students have a handle on how to create team agreements, allow them to discuss among themselves what they think should be included.

Consequences for Violations

An important part of drawing up a group contract is coming up with the consequences for not meeting the team expectations. It's helpful to have a system in which each student is allotted a certain number of warnings or strikes before more serious action is taken. When creating the contract, students should decide how many warnings each group member could get. If someone is off-task or violates the contract, group members are responsible for giving those warnings to each other.

If a student was absent from school and did not check in with other group members, leaving the group unable to work that day, the group should collectively give that student a warning. This isn't an argument or even a confrontation; instead, it is a clear statement recognizing that someone did not uphold the group contract. The student who was absent might not have been aware that they affected the group, but this warning now ensures that they are. It helps prevent resentment and all of the consequences of not communicating issues. When one student receives a warning from the group, it is a wake-up call to collaborate better and work harder. This usually results in no further issues.

Conflict Remediation

Sometimes a student keeps violating the team agreements and uses up all of their warnings. This results in a more serious action, which is up for the teacher to decide. In my classes, it's usually a sit-down meeting with me, the teacher. Meeting with a teacher is the result of multiple warnings and can never be used as a first option. Students need to learn how to manage issues with each other and cannot always turn to authority to resolve them.

This is true in the workplace as well. Going to a manager with every grievance one has about someone else is not efficient. It's a waste of the manager's time, and probably a waste of the employees' time as well.

At this meeting, I allow both sides to share their grievances and defenses, letting group members air out their problems. I spend this time mainly listening, and quite often the conversation goes like this:

"He hasn't done any work."

"That's because no one told me what to do!"

"We talked about what to do as a group, and you were on your phone!"

"That's because you wouldn't listen to my ideas anyway!"

The teacher should mainly listen during this part, because sometimes groups just need the space to vent. It's easy to want to jump in and try to solve the problem, but conflict resolution is much more successful when students lead the way. Teachers should be conflict mediators, making sure language and tone do not become disrespectful, and that conversation is moving in a positive direction.

To assist in this, it's extremely helpful to have an *active listening protocol* to guide the discussion. Here's a great example adapted from Emily White and Nancy Mohr:[3]

1. Allow one side to speak for a full two minutes.

     a. During the conversation, maintain eye contact with each other while speaking, but do not say anything.

     b. It is important not to pass judgment on the person speaking, even by reassuring or reaffirming them. You should even avoid nodding your head, making agreeable sounds, like "uh huh," or even, "I get that." This is their time to speak and share their side of the story.

2. When they finish, wait ten seconds and then rephrase what they said, using the sentence starter, "What I heard you say is…"

3. Wait for confirmation or explanation.

4. Ask one follow-up question.

5. Switch.

Having a strict protocol for students to follow ensures that everyone is heard, and no one leaves the conversation feeling like they were disrespected. Once all of the grievances have been laid bare, try to find a way to get the group working together again. Say something like, "It sounds like you guys are frustrated because he isn't working, and he is frustrated because no one is listening to his ideas. What do you think needs to happen to get this group back on track?"

Students then come up with a plan, often agreeing to a fresh start, and the group can get back to work. Most of the time, and I mean the vast majority of the time, this conflict remediation is successful. Most students just need to be made aware that their actions are affecting everyone else, and they will do everything they can to remedy that. We desire peace, and sometimes we have to confront the problem to achieve it. Some of the best collaboration I have ever witnessed came after one of these heart-to-heart conversations. Everyone feels heard and valued, and as a result, works harder and with more passion.

Joint Write-Ups

Another way to facilitate remediation is to have students first create a joint write-up of the situation that is delivered to the teacher to review before dealing with the group's issue. As a group, students write a description of the problem, and everyone is allowed to add whatever they'd like to the document. The accusers and the accused can describe the collaboration struggles however they'd like. In doing this, students are forced to confront the issues with each other, eliminating any mystery about why there is frustration and discord in the group. In many cases, by systematically documenting the problem before meeting with the teacher, students will come to an understanding with each other and can continue the work without even needing to have the teacher address it.

This joint write-up process uses collaboration to solve collaboration issues! By working together to create the document for the teacher, students have to communicate and voice their problems with each other. As with the teacher remediation, this is usually all that is necessary to get teams back on track.

Here's an idea for what to include on the Joint Write-Up forms.

Group member names: _____

Description of issue: _____

Steps taken to resolve the issue: _____

Notes from individuals:

(Name)_____:_____

(Name)_____:_____

(Name)_____:_____

(Name)_____:_____

 Get the Joint Write-Ups template in the Collaborative Classroom Toolkit at trevormuir.com/resources.

Firing a Group Member

Sometimes students who have failed to meet group expectations do not agree to collaborate and change their actions. In such instances in my classroom, they can be fired from the group. This means they are removed from the group setting and must complete the entire project individually. They cannot use any of the resources gathered from the groups that they were in, but they still have the same deadline and expectations as everyone else. Students who are fired from their groups will be assessed according to the same standard as their peers. When assessed for collaboration, which we'll talk about in Chapter 5, this student will receive a zero because they clearly demonstrated their inability to collaborate.

I also call their moms.

Pretty harsh, isn't it?

It should be noted that this is not a punishment but a natural consequence for negative actions. These are similar actions to those one would see in the workforce if they were not collaborating and producing well (except maybe for calling one's parents—not sure that technique happens as much in the career world).

I make my students very aware of the firing process at the beginning of the school year when we talk about accountability. I want everyone to understand that the group contract should be taken seriously, and that there are consequences for not abiding by it. The reality is, students do not want to be fired from their group, and they do not want to have to complete an entire project on their own. They learn how to collaborate and hold each other accountable.

This is why, in my entire career, I've seen maybe five students fired from their groups. The group contract is not an excuse for students to fire each other but actually a tool to prevent it. They should access it throughout a group project, returning to their agreements and reminding each other of them when they are violated.

The contract is not just a bit of minutia at the beginning of a project. It is the foundation for accountability to ensure that project's success. This is why I have my students sign their names to it after its completion. They are signing a covenant to work together to achieve the best possible outcomes.

Developing a Culture of Accountability

Accountability cannot be forced on students. It can be strongly recommended and even modeled, but accountability is an act of will. Students must see the value in it and how it serves such a crucial purpose to use it. This is why, no matter how much I emphasize the use of group contracts, joint write-ups, and project management logs at the beginning of the year and throughout, I still have students tell me at the end of projects that someone in their group did not work.

When teams use group contracts, you can then ask, "How many warnings did you give them? How many conversations did you have with this person? How come I'm just hearing about this issue at the very end of the project?"

You can then have the conversation with the student about why holding each other accountable is so important and why tools such as the group contract or PML can be so useful.

Accountability has to be woven into the class culture. This starts with teaching accountability, but also with allowing experience to teach it as well.

At the beginning of every school year, when I have students fill out group contracts for the first time, I ask them how many warnings someone in your group should be allowed before they are sent to the teacher to be potentially fired. Most groups record that each student will receive approximately ten warnings before a meeting with me, the teacher.

Then the project begins, team agreements are violated, and it goes something like this:

"You didn't work today; here's a warning."

"You didn't check in when you were absent; here's a warning."

"You've been on your phone all morning; here's a warning."

"You slept all class while we worked; here's a warning."

"You won't stop using your headphones when we are collaborating; here's a warning." Etc.

Students learn in that first project that allowing ten warnings is not being generous; it's being unwise. Needless to say, by the next project, kids start writing down in their group contracts that they are not giving out any warnings, and that you can be fired for your first offense! This is where I try to redirect a little and emphasize grace and second chances.

The point is, reality and experiences teach them accountability. If one group member is not contributing, it can have a dramatic effect on the rest of the group. Sometimes this point needs to be learned through experience. Students will see how much better group work can be when they use the tools available to them to hold each other, and themselves, accountable.

It's also helpful to model this early on and as needed. Teachers can suggest phrases to use when addressing someone. They can share stories of when they have had to do it in their own life and profession. Teachers should be open to students expressing their frustrations and provide counsel on how to talk about them with someone. More than anything, teachers should emphasize the purpose for accountability over and over.

Teammate accountability can become a part of class culture, and when it does, the need for it becomes less and less. As students learn the natural consequence of not contributing to a group's effort, they adjust and work better in their teams. It takes effort and some difficult experiences to build this culture, but the benefit makes it worth it.

Students are no longer left in frustration as one group member plays video games while everyone else works. They now know how to respectfully ask them to stop because they are violating the agreed-upon norms set at the beginning of the project.

This makes collaboration possible. And the more students do it, the better they will become at it. You will see the advantages right before your eyes in your classroom, but more importantly, students will see it the rest of their lives. From group projects in college, to working in an increasingly diverse and collaborative workplace, students will know how to have those conversations to ensure that everyone is working to their full potential.

Reflection

1. When you were a student, were you more prone to being a hog or a log?
2. When was a time you have successfully held someone else accountable for their work? How did it feel afterward?
3. How can you improve your conflict remediation skills?
4. What does it mean for students to own the conflicts happening in their groups?

Take Action

Customize the Group Contract to fit your group of students.

#CollaborativeClassroom

CHAPTER 4

TEACHING ADAPTABILITY

It is not the strongest of the species that survives, nor the most intelligent. It is the one that is most adaptable to change.

—Charles Darwin

My wife's grandfather returned home from World War II in 1946 and started working as an electrician at a brass factory. Although his roles and duties changed over time, he stayed with that company, in the same factory, for the next forty years until he retired. Forty years with most of the same people and the same setting, doing the same tasks.

This is what many people from his generation experienced. The economy grew under stable and predictable jobs, and school was a place to learn how to thrive in this environment.

Fast forward seventy years, and the average American has twelve different jobs throughout a lifetime. According to a 2018 report from the Bureau of Labor Statistics, today's workers hold a specific job for an average of four years.[1] Younger workers, such as millennials, have approximately five different jobs before they even turn thirty.

The days of cashing out a pension after forty years of loyalty are over.

Whether you view this as a negative or a positive, it is a reality that isn't likely to change anytime soon. The independent research firm Edelman Intelligence reports that there are currently 53.7 million freelancers in America, and across the country, 37 percent of all workers are employed on a contract basis.[2] Employment looks drastically different than it did in even the recent past. Stephanie Kasriel, the CEO of the freelancing firm Upwork, says, "Professionals are not only turning away from traditional employment; once they do, most have no desire to go back. [They are] increasingly building flexible careers on their own terms, based on their passions, desired lifestyle and access to a much broader pool of opportunities than ever before in history."[2] The rigid hierarchies and familiarity of the workforce is increasingly becoming a thing of the past.

This freelance work culture, whether a person in it is self-employed or job-hops every few years, means that people are constantly working with new people in different systems. To do so, they have to be able to adapt. They need to know how to enter an unfamiliar ecosystem, join the culture there, and thrive right away.

When school looks like the outdated model of employment based on a standard hierarchy of management (teachers) and employees (students), we are doing students a disservice. The workforce is looking less and less like this, and students need to be introduced to the new work model. Students need to learn adaptability and how to assimilate and thrive in new environments with new people and new challenges.

If students do not struggle through these challenges in school, they will inevitably face them in the workforce, where there is less room for grace and correction. According to research by Barclays Life Skills, "60 percent [of employers] report that adaptability has become more important during the previous decade; 20 percent, meanwhile, say that adaptability is lacking among recruits, and only 8 percent actually provide specific training for this."[3]

Assign Work That Requires Agility

Being adaptable is its own challenge. When students are forced out of the norm and made to interact with peers outside of their comfort zones, they lose the stability and security they have always known in school. Although many students do not enjoy the individual model of school, and certainly do not thrive in it, it is familiar, and they are used to it. This is why having a collaborative classroom can create friction at first. Students do not possess the skills needed to adapt to new people and challenges, which is all the more reason to create an environment that requires adaptability.

When schoolwork is predictable and the only aspect of it that changes is the subject matter, students do not have to be agile or adaptable. Students need to be regularly forced out of their comfort zones. Although students might want to work with their friends and the people they are comfortable with, collaborating with new people can have a much greater impact on the project's success as well as students' individual growth. When students are obligated to work with new people, have and resolve conflicts with unfamiliar peers, and build professional relationships with peers outside of their friend groups, they are forced to be agile and adaptable.

Another way to build agility and adaptability is to regularly rotate tasks that students work on in collaborative groups. If one student has a propensity toward technology and is usually the one to edit videos, create graphics, conduct research, or do whatever else involves a computer, challenge that student to give that role to someone else for a specific project. Maybe even require it. You might be met with frustration at first because that student is comfortable with a technology role, and the rest of the group wants them to have it as well, but this will force a different student to adapt and learn a new skill.

My high school students once worked in pairs to create illustrated children's books to present at a local elementary school. The primary tasks included writing, editing, and illustrating. Before the project, I had students fill out a survey indicating which task they were most comfortable doing—writing or illustrating. Once they found out what the project was, I announced they had to take on the opposite role of what they indicated on the survey.

As you can imagine, my students were not very happy with me about this. My artsy students wanted to design the pictures, and my writers wanted to write the stories. Now they had to do a new task that they were not as comfortable with. Students initially told me that the books wouldn't be any good because of how I was assigning roles. "Mr. Muir, I'm terrible at drawing. This is going to look like garbage."

I responded, "Who says you have to draw the books?"

This got students thinking deeper about how they wanted to create images for the story. Some came up with the idea to cut out pictures from magazines and paste them into the book. Others figured out how to use Photoshop and doctored pictures off of the internet. And still others practiced drawing and found out they were not "terrible" at it.

This assignment forced students to adapt.

One of the best ways to engage those students in class is to use their skills in schoolwork. A critique of choosing students' roles for a collaborative project like this could be that it stifles their own engagement by not using their abilities. The answer to this is ensuring that the project remains collaborative.

Just because students have different roles and tasks in a project does not mean that they do not get to have input on each other's work. Schedule time in class for students to provide consulting to each other. If working on a project such as the children's book, give students five minutes at the end of project work time to review each other's work. Consider this structure:

1. Review the work.
2. Point out what they like about it.
3. Suggest what can be done to improve it.

This allows students to return to work that is more comfortable to them and to exercise their stronger skillset a bit. It honors a student's expertise while also giving them a new way to express themselves outside of the primary task. Allowing for this consulting time also prevents the project from being one of those individual projects in which each student completes a task and combines it at the end of a project.

It's important to find opportunities for students to have primary tasks in areas that align with their skillsets, but it's also vital to look for experiences that stretch them and force them to step out of their comfort zones. This is what creates moments that require them to adapt.

Emphasize Courage and Confidence

My students once had a project in which they created presentations based on interviews that they conducted with people they considered heroes. These presentations would be displayed at a public event at the local library, and one of the components was creating a podcast telling the hero's story. For this project, I pulled the old "Survey-and-Switch" technique and required students to work on unfamiliar tasks. One student named Drew was given the podcast task and begged me to let him work on something else. He said he hated working with computers and had no idea how to record and edit a podcast.

I saw this as the perfect opportunity for him to learn and adapt. Therefore, I required Drew to keep the podcast role and to let me know if he needed any help.

A couple of times throughout the project, I sat with Drew and showed him a few basics for editing audio and directed him toward YouTube tutorials. I believed he was equipped to complete his tasks for his group.

On the day of the presentation, when I had students set up their work at the library for the event, Drew's group was missing the podcast, and Drew was suspiciously absent from school that day. The show went on without him, but that group's podcast was missing from the presentation.

The next day, when Drew was back in class and I found out his podcast wasn't even finished, I confronted him about his absence from school on such an important day of class.

And I wasn't very nice about it.

I asked Drew, in front of the class, how he could do that to his group: "Did you not think about how they would be affected by your failure to complete the work? How could you let your laziness get in the way of such an important project?" I thought I was emphasizing the importance of accountability with Drew, but as I was addressing him, I saw him sink further and further into his seat. I realized mid-sentence that I was shaming the kid. I could see in his eyes that he was embarrassed, and so was everyone else in the room.

After class I asked Drew to stay behind, and I apologized for how I addressed him publicly the way I did. I said that while I was disappointed about the project, I did not handle it well at all. I apologized for embarrassing him and promised that I would do better next time. Drew was taken aback by this vulnerable moment. He then apologized for his lack of work on the project and explained that he was just so scared of the podcast not turning out well that he just didn't submit it. Drew explained that he has always been scared of trying new things and gets anxiety at the mere thought of others seeing him fail. He decided he'd rather get a poor grade than a poor reaction to his work.

On reviewing Drew's work, I saw that his planning was excellent, and he had all the components to complete the project. It was the final step of recording that he failed to complete. This was the part of the project that was new territory for him. His lack of confidence in himself froze his work.

According to a survey conducted for entrepreneur.com,[4] lacking confidence is one of the key reasons young people get fired from their jobs. Not having the courage to make firm decisions and take concrete action leads to a lack of productivity. One of the key components in students becoming adaptable is instilling personal confidence and courage in them.

Build Positive Relationships

Lynn Taylor, workplace expert and author of *Tame Your Terrible Office Tyrant,*[5] says, "The most common reason that employees lose confidence is very simply because of a bad relationship with their boss. That insecurity will last as long as the relationship is strained." Anyone who has had this type of relationship with a principal or superintendent knows exactly what Taylor is talking about. When teachers do not feel trusted to make decisions or learn from failures, the response is often to shut down, halting progress.

When I had a principal who did not trust me and seemingly questioned every move I made in the classroom, I stopped making those moves. I quit dressing up in costumes when teaching history lessons for fear of being labeled as unprofessional by my boss. I scaled down the scope of the projects I did with students because I feared something would go wrong and I would face punishment. I no longer brought in guest speakers to my class because I couldn't control every word they said, and my boss made it clear that teachers should control every word said to students.

I lost confidence in myself as a teacher, and as a result, became a dramatically worse one. This ended in me leaving that school and going somewhere I could be confident again.

The same is true for students. If there is a strained relationship between them and their teachers, this will affect their confidence and quality of work in class. Except students usually do not have the option of finding a better school and teacher.

This is why positive student relationships are so crucial. If a student knows they will not be scorned for their mistakes, and that a teacher's primary motivation is helping them succeed, they will not feel the same trepidation at trying new things.

From asking personal questions, to having class time every day dedicated to nonacademic discussion, to having an open-door policy to listen when students need to be listened to, the building of these strong relationships has immense value.

I think this is part of the reason Drew did not complete the podcast assignment. It wasn't that he was being lazy; his outlining work showed otherwise. Drew did not have the personal confidence in himself and was afraid of how his peers and boss (me) would react to his work. Interestingly, after the incident in which I apologized for addressing him the way I did in front of the class, Drew and I formed a new relationship. My vulnerability opened the doors to Drew trusting me, and for the rest of the year I saw a dramatic increase in the quality and quantity of work Drew turned in.

Don't Micromanage

Every teacher, and really every leader, has felt the temptation to micromanage at times. When we see work that is being done inefficiently, or even just not being completed the way we would do it, it can seem like the best solution is to interject and offer advice or directions. However, micromanaging, whether intentional or not, is one of the top confidence killers. It sends the message to students that we do not trust them to complete the task correctly. Helene Lerner, author of *The Confidence Myth*,[6] says that a supervisor micromanaging "has more to do with how that person feels about him or herself, not you."

The tendency to micromanage is rooted in pressure and a fear of failure. If students do not complete the task correctly or do not learn what we intend for them to learn, teachers are held accountable. Although this sadly can be true, it's also true that if a task is only completed because of the constant hovering of the teacher, students probably did not learn what they were intended to learn anyway. The same can be said of the manager who micromanages their employees; the employees' impact is minimalized because the task really could have just been completed by the manager themselves.

Here are a few ways to avoid micromanaging and instill confidence in your students:

- Let them delegate tasks.
- Instead of telling students in collaborative groups who is doing what, let them do so. You might give stipulations such as "You must adopt an unfamiliar role" or "I will approve the roles once they are decided," but ultimately give the control to them. This shows you trust them with a very important task.
- Give information up front and have designated check-in times.
- Rather than checking in with students at random times and when they do not expect it, structure the time you assess and receive status updates. This will reduce anxiety, because students will not always be looking over their shoulders. If students need help, they can approach you, and you can determine whether they need help at scheduled checkpoints. In the meantime, students are trusted to work independently.
- Make students managers.
- Empower students with leadership roles within their groups. This can be a rotating position, but give every student the chance to be a team leader. They can be the point-person with the teacher, lead discussions, delegate roles, have extra accountability for the final product, and be trusted to motivate group members to do their best work. This leadership role is usually held by the teacher, but empowering students to have it is an effective way to build confidence and develop leadership skills.

- Use "I Wonder" language:
  - Our words have power, and the ones we use to address students can have an impact on their confidence. Instead of using phrases such as "Do this" or "You need to," try saying, "I wonder?" For example: "I wonder if there is a way to solve this problem?" or "I wonder if using a black background hides the font?" or "I wonder if it's possible to get all of those tasks completed before the deadline?"

Teachers still need to give direction and lend their expertise, but this can be done in a way that is less micromanaging and more giving thoughts and sharing suggestions.

Modeling Adaptability

Perhaps one of the most effective ways to develop adaptability and agility in your students is to model it yourself. Any educator in any level of the school system knows that there is rarely a day that looks the same as the last. Whether it's fire alarms, absent students, surprise administrator visits, downed Wi-Fi, baby goats on the loose (this actually happened in my class), student outbursts, or power outages, being a teacher requires adaptability.

Teachers should be vocal about when they are forced to adapt in different situations. If the Wi-Fi is out and your internet-based lesson is no longer possible, let students in on your thought process as you come up with an alternative lesson. If you make the decision to do a similar activity on paper, make students aware of how you came to that conclusion, where you got the idea, and why you think it will still be worthwhile.

If you are a teacher, chances are you are already adaptable. It would be hard to make it in this profession if you were not. Way more than once I have arrived to speak at a conference or workshop with teachers and take the stage, only to find out the microphone I was given had dead batteries. Or the projector bulb burned out. Or one time, I was to give a keynote in a gymnasium in eastern Ohio and arrived to find out the school had scheduled a blood drive in that same gymnasium at the same exact time! The superintendent who hired me apologized for the inconvenience, and then gave me the microphone to give my keynote anyway while a bunch of nurses drew blood from townspeople in the back of the gym.

At the height of my keynote, I told an epic story to the crowd. I was letting my words tell the story (but even more, the sound and inflection in my voice), and I became louder and louder as I was reaching its climax. Everyone in the gymnasium was on the edge of their seats as the suspense grew, and just as I was reaching the pivotal moment in the story, a nurse stomped up to me on the stage and said, "You are being too loud! I'm trying to work back here!"

Well, this is awkward.

It was like she poked a hole in my hot air balloon that was climbing into the clouds, and it quickly deflated and crashed back to earth. I said "sorry" to the nurse because I had a few hundred people in front of me and I didn't want them to hear what I really wanted to say. They all stared at me with pursed smiles on their faces as I tried to tell the rest of the story. But there was no way I was getting that energy back, and certainly no way I could get the crowd back on the edges of their seats. I stopped the story, looked at the audience and said, "Has anyone here been in the middle of a really great lesson only to have it disrupted at the very best part?"

The place erupted in a resounding, "YES!"

If this embarrassing disruption had happened anywhere else, I probably would have been mortified. My crowd was made up of teachers, however, and teachers know all about disruptions and adapting on the spot. We know all about ringing cell phones, unplanned assemblies, unexpected profanities in videos we show, flatulence and the laughter that follows, tornado drills in the middle of lessons, canceled guest visits, getting sick and going to work anyway, students on the edge of mental breakdowns, and all of the other unexpected events that require agility.

Teachers are the perfect professionals to show students how to do it as well. Don't keep your ability to adapt a secret. Wear that superpower on your sleeve, modeling how to deal with adversity so your students can do it as well.

Encouraging a Growth Mindset

Carol Dweck's seminal book, *Mindset: The New Psychology of Success,*[7] is about growth mindset and what can be accomplished through effort when we believe that we are capable of growing and improving. Rather than a "fixed mindset," which assumes that people's knowledge, skills, and creativity are givens or capped, Dweck says a "growth mindset is the realization that nothing is fixed, and everyone can improve. With this mindset, challenges, obstacles, and failures are actually experiences to launch us into undiscovered, abundant new lands."

Struggle is the means for growth, and this is something that needs to be made abundantly clear to students. There is no such thing as perfect collaboration. The process of sharing ideas, pressure, and tasks with other people is way too complicated for that. Therefore, when students encounter the first signs of struggle in group work, the temptation is to retreat and declare that they're "not good at it" or that "they hate group projects." These types of statements would be classified under a fixed mindset and the assumption that some people are more apt for collaboration than others. And this fixed mindset travels with students beyond their school years and into the workplace, where they believe they are not collaborators simply because they've struggled with collaborating in the past.

Teachers in a collaborative classroom need to be transparent about the struggle students might expect to face. However, these struggles will make them better collaborators if they are embraced.

One of the ways to build this growth mindset is to read stories that feature characters who learn through failure. From reading these stories and having an explicit discussion afterward about growing through adversity, students can begin to apply these principles to their own lives. For nonfiction, use any text or example that features failure and growth. Share the story of Steve Jobs getting fired from Apple, Michael Jordan not making the varsity basketball team, an article about the struggles of the Apollo missions, or even a story from your own life (plenty to pull from here for myself).

There are also many great fiction books that deal with the growth mindset concept. Some elementary examples are *Beautiful Oops* by Barney Saltzberg,[8] *The Dot* by Peter H. Reynolds,[9] and *The Girl Who Never Makes Mistakes* by Gary M. Rubinstein and Mark Pett.[10] At the secondary level, options include *Island of the Blue Dolphins* by Scott O'Dell,[11] *The Watsons Go to Birmingham—1963* by Christopher Paul Curtis,[12] and *Holes* by Louis Sachar.[13]

Another way to teach students to embrace growth mindset and continual growth is by using and requiring intentional "growth mindset language" in your classroom. Ban the phrases "I can't," "I'm not good at," and "I don't like" from your classroom! Or if you do allow them, make sure they're always followed by the word "yet." I can't solve this problem *yet*. I am not good at grammar *yet*. I can't understand Shakespeare *yet*. Language has power, and the more this idea is reinforced, the more students will adopt it.

Students get really annoyed with me because I require this language. When they let a sentence like "I can't figure this out" slip, they immediately look up at me, roll their eyes, and then say "yet." I take pride in annoying my students this way! I want them to believe the scientifically proven fact that their brains are malleable and are capable of far more than they usually give themselves credit for. I want them to see the value of putting in the extra effort, because it really will pay off. I reinforce this point every chance I get, and this comes with a lot of eye rolls, but also a lot of use of the word "yet" from my students.

This also means shifting the language you use as an educator. When a student experiences failure, instead of saying, "This is what went wrong," say, "What can be done differently next time?" Or, ask what a student learned through an experience and identify any success they might have had along the way. This intentionality in how we speak to students will help coach them through hurdles while conditioning them to develop a growth mindset.

Rather than avoiding challenges, fleeing from obstacles, and deeming effort worthless because of it, students can be conditioned to believe that adversity partners success. When they no longer fear struggle, but embrace it, they are free to enter new and unfamiliar situations and learn to thrive in them. Or another way of putting it: they become adaptable.

Reflection

1. Speaking of an evolving workforce, how has your career in education changed while you've been in it?
2. How have you had to adapt?
3. What does courage look like for you?
4. What does courage look like for your students?
5. When do you feel smart—when you're doing something flawlessly or when you're learning something new?

Take Action

Make a list of regular instances in which you have to adapt and work on the fly.

Now devise how you can make those instances learning moments for your students.

#CollaborativeClassroom

CHAPTER 5

ASSESSING COLLABORATION

Do the one thing you think you cannot do. Fail at it. Try again. Do better the second time. The only people who never tumble are those who never mount the high wire. This is your moment. Own it.

—Oprah Winfrey

n my first year of teaching, Megan came to me on the second-to-last day of a month-long project with a bright red face and tears streaming down her cheeks.

"What's wrong, Megan? Are you okay?" I asked her. I thought she'd just heard terrible news. She was visibly distressed and had trouble getting her words out.

She finally composed herself enough to say, "I ca- I ca- I can't go another day working with this group!"

I responded, "Oh, is that it? Well it's not a big deal, Megan. There's only one day left of the project. Do you think you can make it one more day?"

Rookie mistake.

Megan lost any composure she had left and screamed at me in front of the class that I clearly did not understand her, how bad her group was, and in very direct words how horrible my class was. She then stormed out of my classroom and headed down to the office to have her mom pick her up from school.

Yikes. What just happened here?

After a little reflection, and having been married for ten years now, I think part of the issue was that no one wants to be told their problems are "not a big deal" and then to be immediately offered a solution. (This wasn't the only time I've been taught this lesson.)

I also learned that this group had some serious collaboration issues that should have been addressed much earlier than the last day of the project. But I had no idea that her group was struggling. Every time I walked by them or stopped to check in during collaboration time, they seemed to be on task. All of their assignments were submitted on time, and I did not learn of any group struggles or warnings being given out. From the outside, there was no group conflict.

My perception was clearly off.

After talking to Megan the next day (along with her mother and my principal), I learned that Megan was bearing most of the weight of the project. She was conducting most of the research, completing the collaborative assignments, and doing all of this while trying to manage group members who would rather play Minecraft than contribute.

Megan obviously struggled with holding her group members accountable, and there are tools and processes to help students with this important piece of collaboration (see Chapter 3). This instance also made it abundantly clear to me how easy it is to overlook group conflict and collaboration issues throughout a project or activity.

Simply relying on the eye test to gauge how successfully a team is collaborating is insufficient. Appearances can be deceiving, especially when students do not know how to advocate for themselves yet and voice their problems. The truth is, if Megan had never had her outburst, I would have thought her group was fine. The assignments were turned in, and the project was completed. I wouldn't have known that it was all done by an individual rather than a group.

This raises the question: how often are students struggling with collaboration and their teachers and instructors are failing to realize it?

Use Formative Assessments

The key to identifying collaboration struggles and resolving them requires the same solution for when students struggle with understanding content: formative assessments. Formative assessments are a means to evaluate a student's comprehension of a subject or skill; they are used by an educator to determine further instruction and guidance needed to help that student achieve mastery. Formative assessments move the focus and emphasis of work from grades to mastery. Grading becomes a continuous process, indicating where improvement is needed so students gain proficiency.

In a traditional class, grades are treated as rewards or penalties for the work students do. However, when assessments are used formatively, they serve the sole purpose of improving student work. Like the use of formative assessments to improve a student's mastery working with polynomials or the correct usage of semicolons, they are needed for collaborative skill building.

Teachers in a collaborative classroom should constantly be assessing student collaboration throughout an extended assignment or project. There are three important reasons for this. First, formative assessments for collaboration help put out fires before they get out of control. Teachers serve as mediators in their classrooms and provide wisdom and guidance that their students need. Therefore, the instructor has to have their finger on the pulse at all times to help groups work through issues. Assessments can serve as indicators of growing tensions within groups.

The second reason for collaboration assessments is to help instructors know how to adjust instruction to help students grow in skill. Like my example earlier, I thought the collaborative activities I had for the project were serving my students well. They actually weren't, leaving Megan frustrated and burned out. Strong formative assessments throughout the project can let the teacher know whether students are effectively collaborating or whether adjustments are needed.

Put Collaboration in the Gradebook

The third reason for collaborative assessments follows a bit more along the traditional route of grading. The fact is, some students are motivated by achievements, which is why those students often ignore the group aspect of group work to complete assignments and get their desired grade. If it's not graded, it's not important. We know this to be untrue, but school culture says otherwise. Content work often takes precedence over the "soft skills," which include collaboration.

Part of putting these soft skills on equal footing, or at least near-equal, is to measure growth for these skills as well. Essentially, one's ability to collaborate should go in the gradebook! Otherwise, what message are we sending to students about the importance of this skill? Students should each have a collaboration grade at the end of a semester that reflects their ability to work with others.

Before anti-graders slam this book shut and write a one-star review on Amazon, let me add this. The grade should be malleable and can always improve as the students grow and can demonstrate that growth. If at the beginning of a semester, a student is constantly getting warnings from their group members and earns a 70 percent for collaboration in the first project (more on how to assess this in a minute), that grade demonstrates their ability to collaborate at that specific point in time. However, as the year progresses, and students get additional opportunities to become more proficient at collaboration, and then can demonstrate that, then the gradebook should reflect it.

I've known many intelligent, high-achieving students who, early in the year, have no idea how to collaborate. They turn in excellent individual work, but when it comes to group activities, they are collaboratively illiterate. Using collaborative assessments, the teacher can give a grade to reflect this. And these grades can get those students' attention really quick!

"Teacher! I've never received below a B in my life! Why are you doing this to me?!"

And the teacher's response can be, "And you don't have to get a B. During the next group project, work on _____ to improve collaboration and you will earn a new grade."

In a true collaborative classroom, this collaboration grade should not be the primary motivator for students. The creative power of collaboration and the productivity that can come from it should be what define the collaboration culture of a classroom. However, having a summative grade can help. It demonstrates that collaboration is valued just like the content of the class is. It also doesn't allow students to decide not to be collaborative. It's an accountability tool and helps keep the slackers from slacking and the takeover students from doing all the work.

It's no different from how collaboration is treated in industry. Strong collaboration is rewarded with success, and poor teamwork results in consequences.

Assessing Collaborative Activities

Figuring out the purpose of any assessment is crucial before creating and using it with students. Is it a formative assessment designed to be used as an indicator of a student's progress and need for further practice and instruction? Is the assessment summative and given to provide a record of their progress and to determine their proficiency?

Once this is determined, the teacher can determine what skills to assess and the tools to use for it. However, regardless of the purpose, the assessment is always focused on an individual's ability to contribute to a team and their development of collaborative skills. Remember, the purpose of collaboration is for each team member's personal success to contribute to the overall success of their group. Collaborative assessments should be measuring that personal success.

One of the greatest fears of students and parents alike concerning group work is that the whole group will be graded the same; if one student slacks and does not contribute to the group, then everyone's grade will suffer. The best way to alleviate that fear is to emphasize that collaboration is not assessed that way. Accurate collaborative assessments focus on the individual, so that the individual is strengthened and can then contribute to the group.

Here are assessment tools and resources that can be used to strengthen individual collaboration skills:

Collaboration Rubric

The collaboration rubric is a tool to give students clear expectations for their work in groups. It outlines what strong and weak collaboration looks like and gives students an indication of where their skillset is at a given time. A teacher can use the rubric for any group activity. However, it is important that the focus of the rubric is not on the specific task groups are accomplishing, but rather on the student's demonstration of a collaborative skill in completing that task.

If students were assigned to read an article as a group and then create some type of visual to demonstrate their understanding of the content, the rubric is not evaluating the effectiveness of the visual or whatever the group created. The rubric is assessing each student's contribution to the project and the group as a whole. Did the student manage their time well? Did they listen and respond to their teammates respectfully? Did the student contribute to the creation of the final product?

The actual visual, the final product, will be assessed separately. The collaboration rubric should use wording that serves to evaluate collaboration skills and proficiency.

This is an example of a collaborative rubric:

The Collaborative Classroom Collaboration Rubric

Student Proficiency	Undeveloped	Developing	Accomplished	Advanced
Group Communication	Little if any talking with group. Not actively listening to the speaker. Body language does not reflect engagement.	Uses voice, body language, and listening to communicate most of the time.	Voices opinions and ideas throughout the task. Voice, body, and mind are fully engaged when speaking and listening.	Additionally, uses energy, patience, and inquiry to encourage group members to communicate as well.
Role	Does not know role in the collaborative task.	Knows role, but relies on team members to assign and clarify it.	Knows own role and also the role of other team members. Uses roles of each individual to maximize collaboration.	Additionally, can assign self roles based on own strengths and weaknesses.
Contribution of Ideas	Did not contribute ideas that helped the group achieve success.	Shares ideas and acknowledges others'. However, some ideas lack detail and support.	Contributes ideas to the group and has strong reasoning and support to justify the use of those ideas.	Along with own ideas, builds on others' ideas and incorporates them in the final product.
Self Advocacy	Does not seek assistance from group when necessary.	Asks questions and for assistance from group members as a last resort.	Confidently seeks help from group members whenever necessary.	Additionally, asks others if they need assistance throughout the task.
Work Ethic	Completes few if any of the assigned tasks. Often off-task.	Completes most tasks by the deadline. Mostly on-task.	Completes all tasks by the deadline, and the work is quality and adds significantly to the group's effort.	Along with completing own work, inspires and leads group members to work hard and meet deadlines.

The Collaborative Classroom

 Get the Collaborative Rubric in The Collaborative Classroom Toolkit at trevormuir.com/resources.

This rubric could be used to evaluate a student's entire collaborative effort on a group assignment, or just a specific trait during their work. If students were making a slideshow as a group, you could choose to just focus on a student's communication skills. Only score that part of the rubric, and direct all of your attention during that activity to their ability to talk, listen, and use positive body language. The next day you could concentrate on assessing self-advocacy or another category. This makes assessing collaboration more manageable, because you are not trying to assess a topic as broad as collaboration all at once.

A collaboration rubric should meet the needs of your students.

Feel free to use the collaboration rubric I created in any way you see fit. However, some of the most effective rubrics are created with your students' assistance. This gives them voice and agency, and it also ensures that your rubric fits your specific students and their skill levels.

You could use this rubric as a guide to lead a discussion with students about what strong and weak collaboration looks like and how it should be assessed. Give a writing activity about what minimal and strong work ethics look like. Have a group discussion about self-advocating and seeking help when you need it. Record their responses on a blank rubric. If students are a part of this process, and their language is on the rubric, they will have a better understanding of how they are assessed and what they can do to improve.

Collaboration Exit Ticket

Exit tickets are brief formative assessments to gauge students' understanding at the end of a lesson or activity. While students are wrapping up a collaborative task, give them a short multiple-choice survey asking how they are feeling about their group's cohesiveness and productivity. Keep it short and informal, telling students that their feedback is just for you. Their responses are confidential, and students should not look at each other's. You want their feedback to be sincere so that you can learn from it and make adjustments.

Here's an example:

1. How I'm feeling about my group's collaboration today:

    1—Terrible. We did not work well today.

    2—Not great, but we accomplished some of our goals.

    3—Pretty good. We worked well and mostly stayed on task.

    4—Excellent. We worked great together and accomplished our goals.

2. How I feel about my personal contribution to the group today:

    1—Not great. I did little to assist the group.

    2—Okay, but I mostly worked alone.

    3—Pretty good. I did what was expected and completed my tasks.

    4—Excellent. I contributed and helped my teammates contribute as well.

3. My collaboration skills have improved compared with the last collaborative activity

    1—Yes

    2—No

This exit ticket can be printed off and collected from students at the end of class, or you could use a program such as Google Forms to gather this information. Remember that it is purely a formative assessment. Make sure students know this, so that they are not worried about a grade and give honest feedback. This brief survey at the end of an activity can provide you with valuable information to gauge each student's collaboration skills.

Peer and Self-Assessments

Peer and self-assessments are among the most powerful tools in the collaborative assessment arsenal. This assessment is delivered before, during, and after a collaborative project for students to give their own appraisal of themselves as well as their teammates' collaborative progress. The purpose of this is for the teacher and the students to have clarity about how they are progressing collaboratively. Knowing one's strengths and room for growth is essential to moving forward. However, this can only happen if students have intentional time to reflect.

This starts with a pre-assessment before any collaboration takes place. At the beginning of a collaborative project, have students answer the following four questions.

Pre-Collaboration Self-Assessment

1. What is the purpose of group work?

The purpose behind this question is to gauge a student's understanding of why work is being done collaboratively instead of individually. This answer will change and strengthen as students do more collaborative work and see success because of it.

2. How do I feel about contributing ideas to a group?

   a. No confidence. I do not contribute ideas to a group

   b. Uncomfortable, but I can do it

   c. Okay, but not completely comfortable

   d. Very confident

This question gives students a chance to reflect on their own confidence in contributing to a group. Ask students to be honest in their response, and let them know that they will be answering the same question at the end of the project, where they will see whether they have grown in this area at all.

For students who answer with the choice A, the teacher now knows that this student might need extra attention, and the student now has a clear goal to strive for. Again, this clarity is essential to achieve progress.

3. What do I do best in group work?

   a. Leading the team

   b. Being reliable and completing my assigned tasks on time

   c. Holding others accountable

   d. Contributing ideas

   e. Other

This allows learners to identify a collaborative strength that they possess so they can continue to hone it and take advantage of that strength while working in their group. This isn't to say the student cannot be strong in the other listed areas, but being able to identify a specific strength can help them set goals to aim higher and achieve more.

4. What do I need to improve most in group work?

   a. Leading the team

   b. Reliability and completing my assigned tasks on time

   c. Holding others accountable

   d. Contributing ideas

   e. Other

By collecting these pre-assessment data, the teacher and the student can compare their responses not only at the beginning of a collaborative project, but also at the end of a semester and school year. A student might start a project identifying their greatest strength as being their reliability, but then come to find that it is actually their ability to contribute new ideas. A student could start off the year feeling weak in the area of leadership but develop leadership skills from continuous collaborative work and see that as a new strength.

Having regular assessments that ask these four simple questions is a means to measure, record, and reflect on these developments.

 Get the Self-Assessments in The Collaborative Classroom Toolkit at trevormuir.com/resources.

Assessing Your Peers

The peer assessment is when students evaluate their group members' collaborative progress. Anytime there is an extended collaborative activity, meaning a group of students is working together for multiple days or weeks at a time, the peer assessment should be used throughout. Students are asked to evaluate each group member's effort and contribution using a four-point scale. After giving a number score, they need to justify in writing why they gave that score. The assessment can look something like this:

	Communication and Collaboration
0	No Group Involvement
1	Was present by made minimal contributions
2	Contributed to group but was inconsistent
3	Made a solid contribution to the group, but better effort could have been made
4	• Group member gave their best effort every single day of the project. • Communicated well with group members • Notified team members when absent from school • Held others accountable • Made an effort to contribute to the overall project

Names	Communication and Collaboration ranking (0-4)	Explain the ranking you gave
(Your Name)	(Rank you give yourself)	
(Group Member's Name)	(Rank group member)	

Get the Peer Assessment in the Collaborative Classroom Toolkit at trevormuir.com/resources.

Here are the four critical components of the Peer Assessment:

Students remain anonymous to group members.

Whether it's first graders or eleventh graders, the peer assessment can be a sensitive activity for students. The evaluation asks them to be honest and hold their group members accountable for their work. This is why it is vital that student feedback be kept anonymous. The purpose of the assessment is not for students to confront their group members. There are other processes for that (see Chapter 3). This peer assessment is for the instructor to get an idea for how groups feel about collaboration, and for individuals to see how their team members feel. To get the most accurate results, this process should be done anonymously.

Peer assessments should occur at the end of and during the project.

Assigning peer assessments at the end of a collaborative project is great, and it is an effective way to wrap up collaborative work and assess group work. However, if it is only administered at the end, it is a summative assessment and only being used to evaluate the progress of the project.

The peer assessment is a tool to improve skills, and so it should not just be used at the end of a project. It should be given throughout, with students learning from each other how their role in the group is going. In doing so, they can make improvements and not have to wait until the next collaborative project to become a better collaborator.

Peer grades do not go in the gradebook.

As stated earlier, collaboration absolutely belongs in the gradebook. However, it's important to note that the teacher or instructor should be the one to put those grades in, not the students. The peer assessment is a helpful indicator of a student's collaborative competency and should be taken into account when determining the collaboration grade; however, students need to be aware that they are not being graded solely on the feedback of their partners.

The classroom would not be a pleasant place if students believed the reason that they have a D in the gradebook was because a group member gave it to them—especially if there were already issues between group members. The teacher also would not like to get those phone calls from parents asking why their child is being graded by some other kid. (Teachers, can I get an AMEN?)

The peer assessment should be used in conjunction with the other collaboration assessment tools. This allows the teacher to say to students, "There is no point giving your friends a 4 on the rubric to be nice. If they clearly did not deserve a 4, I already know that. They won't be seeing your feedback, so give an honest assessment."

Students should assess themselves as well.

Like the pre-assessment, students should score themselves as well and justify that score. Ask students to be honest with themselves, and remind them that the grade they give will not be the only factor determining their final collaboration grade.

The Peer Assessment can set up powerful learning opportunities for students. For some, it can be a "kick-in-the-butt" and serve as an indicator that they need to improve because their group is not pleased with their work. It isn't uncommon for a student to give himself a 4 on the self-assessment portion, only to have the rest of the group give that student a 1. In these situations, I set up a conference with the student and talk about the feedback on the assessment.

This is why it is so critical to *update* that grade at the end of the project to reflect a student's current proficiency. Often, getting a poor collaboration grade in the middle of a project, especially one that uses peer assessments to determine it, can be what it takes to turn an individual's performance around. The grade is a wake-up call, and quite often students respond positively to it. If they make an effort to grow their collaborative skills, and they are successful the next time they are assessed, the gradebook should reflect that.

The Peer Assessment also can be an affirmation for students, recognizing their progress. People naturally want to be accepted and to get the approval of their peers. For many students, working hard to get a positive response on the Peer Assessment is an effective motivator for students. It reinforces strong collaboration and indicates for students what is working and what should be improved.

Collaboration Is a Process

When I joined the swim team my freshman year of high school, the extent of my skills was the ability to swim around and dive to the bottom. I'd grown up swimming, so I was familiar with it and could definitely handle myself in a pool, but there was no grace to how I moved in the water. My form was not defined, and I didn't stand a chance beating anyone in a race with my hybrid freestyle–doggy-paddle stroke.

This was confirmed in my first swim meet, when I came in dead last in my heat. In the fifty-meter freestyle event, I swam it in about thirty-five seconds. For those not versed in competitive swimming, this is pretty slow. At the time, I was hard on myself for the bad time and for losing the race. But it made sense that I was a slow swimmer because I was new to it! I didn't yet have the proper form and technique. My lungs weren't conditioned yet, and I had to breathe too often. My coaches were new to me and I still had a lot to learn from them.

As I practiced more and more, received more instruction and guidance, and built more muscle, my time started to improve. By the district meet at the end of the season, I placed in my event and swam the fifty-meter freestyle in twenty-five seconds. For my freshman year, twenty-five seconds was my personal best. That thirty-five-second score was discarded. It didn't count anymore because it did not reflect my current swimming and racing ability.

This is how we have to view student collaboration skills. They have to be given many opportunities to collaborate and continually receive feedback on their skills. Only from this feedback and chances to iterate and form new disciplines will students improve in their collaboration skills.

The gradebook should reflect a student's ability to collaborate, but the grade should be flexible and redeemable based on students getting better with practice and reflection. If at the beginning of a project the collaboration rubric shows that a student is undeveloped in their collaborative skills but reflects at the end of the project that they are advanced, then clearly collaborative practice has helped. The collaborative assessments have been effective as well. Therefore, the student's grade should reflect that.

Just like when I got third place at the district swim meet.

Reflection

1. What is the purpose of formative assessments?
2. What do you think the benefits of peer discussions are?
3. What potential issues do you see with peer assessments?
4. How can you adapt the Collaborative Rubric to work for your students?

Take Action

Examine a current unit or project and find opportunities in which students could receive feedback on their collaborative skills.

#CollaborativeClassroom

CHAPTER 6

CREATING EFFECTIVE GROUPS

The only way to learn how to work with different people is by working with different people.

—Trevor Muir

"Teacher, I promise I work so much better when I sit next to her. We're best friends and get along great."

"Teacher, I don't get along with him, so we really shouldn't be in a group together."

"Teacher, can we please pick our groups?! We always do better when we get to pick who we work with."

"Teacher, it's not fair you get to pick our groups!"

As a teacher with a collaborative classroom, I've heard each of these lines more times than I can count. Whenever there is even a hint that students will be working or discussing in groups, there is an immediate rush to ask me whether they can choose who they work with. From day one of the school year, my students beg and plead in utter desperation for me to not use the dreaded seating chart and allow them to sit and work with their friends. Every time, without exception, no matter how much pleading I hear and despite how well the students craft their arguments, regardless of whether they have demonstrated the collaborative skills of honeybees and the focus and diligence of brain surgeons, my answer is always the same: NO!

Maybe I occasionally budge on this and give some choice, but that's not nearly as dramatic as the previous sentence. The truth is, I rarely allow my students, even my fourth-year college students, to choose where they sit in my classroom. And at the beginning of the year, when I am still establishing a collaborative culture, my students are not pleased with this aspect of my class. They assume I am a crotchety old teacher bent on using my power to make their lives miserable by not letting them sit with their friends.

But what students often don't understand, even though I explain it on day one of each school year, is that assigned seating in my classroom is not a punishment. I don't choose collaborative groups as a result of bad behavior, nor as a means of preventing it. I don't assign seats to make taking attendance easier (although it definitely helps) or to make it less complicated passing back schoolwork. My mission isn't to separate friends from each other so that they won't talk during class.

I actually assign seats so that students *will talk* in class.

Promoting Better Communication

When I used to allow students to choose the groups they sat in, they always found their friends or close acquaintances, the people they were comfortable with. Which, of course, makes sense. I do the same thing at staff meetings. Sitting by people you know is easier, and if you are not great at meeting new people or not in the mood for it, it makes sense to stick with the familiar. We gravitate toward security and stability, even if it's not always the best thing for us.

This is evidenced when it comes time for class discussion. Students are not stretched and challenged as much when sharing with the people around them. Because they are surrounded by familiar people, they are either too distracted by their friends to have a meaningful discussion or they feel completely comfortable having a discussion. (I'll explain why this is a problem in a moment.)

The first scenario can be improved through facilitation by the teacher and using different strategies to have strong class discussions (see Chapter 8). From using great discussion stems to making discussion participation a graded assessment, there are other ways to get kids involved in discussion without changing up the seating chart. The second scenario is the main reason I mix up groups. I already know that friends can converse and discuss with each other. That's a skill most kids have down and do not need to practice. Assigning students to groups with people they don't know can create an uncomfortable tension during class discussion. It is essentially asking students to perform public speaking with a three- or four-person audience.

Discussing group work with new people is public speaking practice.

Public speaking is no simple task for a lot of us. In fact, it's many people's greatest fear. I honestly think this is at the heart of why many students have trouble joining class discussions when they are with new people. It's another form of public speaking. That is valuable in almost any career field, and students need to learn how to use it. Creating a space where students are forced to share their thinking with "strangers," or even with kids who are not a part of their inner circle, is a great step toward students feeling comfortable with communicating with larger groups. It requires leaving their comfort zone.

It also can create some very stale conversations at first. And that's okay. In the beginning, students can be apprehensive about sharing with people they don't know and often can have a fear of being judged. If you create a culture in which students are constantly turning to talk to each other and shifting the focus from you, the teacher, to them, the conversations will loosen up. Students will start sharing with kids outside of their friend groups, and they will realize that they are capable of discussing and conversing outside of their comfort zones. This will make them better at holding discussions on their own and better at public speaking.

Choosing Groups for Collaborative Work

This principle applies to all collaborative work students do. Some students might find it easier to hold a friend accountable for laziness or for being overbearing. When students are not paired up with friends, they are forced to learn how to deal with confrontation with acquaintances or strangers. According to the data I mentioned previously, this is what people are asked to constantly do in the modern workforce.

This is challenging, but the challenges build resilience. This resilience and grit simply would not develop if students could just choose who they work with. They have to have the opportunity to learn adaptability.

Does this mean collaborative groups should just be chosen at random?

Of course not!

There should always be a degree of strategy when selecting groups that students will work in. Choosing groups is an intentional process that takes students' skills, personalities, strengths, and weaknesses, and the collaborative task, into account.

This starts with forming groups that are the optimal size.

Optimal Group Size

The first group project I ever had my students work in was in groups of eight.

Eight!

As you can imagine, it was absolute mayhem. The students were constantly off-task, the loudest ones were the only ones heard, the quiet ones were easily drowned out, and the slackers had no problem shirking responsibility and allowing the inevitable go-getters to do all the work.

Such large groups made collaborative classroom management almost impossible. But even if I did have the collaborative culture in place to manage this time effectively, groups of this size tend to break off into sub-groups, and the work becomes compartmentalized, negating the purpose of such a large group.

For the next project, I had students work in pairs. My thinking was: the smaller, the better. There'd be fewer distractions and more focus on the tasks at hand. However, I quickly learned that two-person groups have their own issues. For one, students in pairs cannot accomplish the same amount of work as larger groups. If the adage "Many hands make light work" is true, which is really what this book is about (otherwise, why collaborate?!), then the scale of a project is much smaller with groups of two. A group of that size could not accomplish all of the tasks a true project requires in the small amount of time that is available.

Two-person groups also mean fewer ideas are contributed and fewer skills are brought to a collaborative task. The heart of collaboration is combining skills and experiences to improve outcomes. While two is better than one, it is still limiting.

Patrick Laughlin, a professor at the University of Illinois, conducted a study for the *Princeton Review*[1] in which he gave 760 students a specific problem. He compared the results of students who completed the problem individually with the results of students who worked in groups of two, three, four, and five. He found that the groups of two did not perform any better than the individuals. Groups of three, four, and five, however, all equally outperformed them.

Because three-person groups are the most efficient and easy to manage, you could surmise from this research that the optimal group size is three. There are a number of reasons for this. Groups of three are small enough to remain conversational but large enough to have varying perspectives. Having three people eliminates the issue of groups becoming split on decisions. Three allows for a majority, which makes decision-making smoother.

I've also assigned many four-person groups in my classroom, because certain projects and tasks benefit from larger groups, but I do not ever have more than five students per group, because that's the point at which it becomes ineffective. Part of creating adaptable students is optimizing their collaboration experience whenever possible. They need to see the success that can come from collaboration, and this is helped by having the right-sized groups.

Creating Groups to Meet the Needs of Students

Whether students are doing a full-blown collaborative project, a single assignment, or having a collaborative discussion, intentionality is essential. When creating groups, the teacher should consider these two questions:

1. Will these groups optimize the work that can be accomplished?
2. What do each of my individual students need from the project?

For the first question, we have the actual task in mind. If students are creating a video, how will my group assignments ensure the best possible videos? If students are discussing a chapter of a book, how will these groups make it rich and fruitful?

The task is important and definitely should be considered, but a collaborative classroom is about teaching collaboration, not just using it to achieve. This is why the second question is so vital. Groups should be intentionally created to help students grow.

If you have students who are low-skilled collaborators and could use special assistance, they would likely benefit from being in a group with leaders capable of pushing and motivating them to participate. If you have students who are constantly riding on the coattails of others, it can sometimes be beneficial to place them in groups with other students who do that. By having to work with others who have slacked in the past, they can be forced to rise to the occasion.

This can also lead to a group accomplishing little if anything, as all the slackers continue to slack. Students will see the consequences of their behavior instead of being bailed out by their teammates. This is obviously not a fun way for students to learn this fact, but learning through failure rarely is. As long as those students are given an opportunity to reflect on the experience afterwards, they can grow and learn from it. Group selection is largely about meeting the needs of individuals.

Before a collaborative project, I write every student's name on a card and lay it out on a table. I then put the cards under headings based on student behaviors. The headings might include "strong collaborator," "weak collaborator," "quiet," "talkative," "passive," "aggressive," and so on. The headings can be anything helpful to organize students before creating groups for a specific task or project. I should note that this process is absolutely confidential from the students. Students carrying these labels or thinking their teacher does is not helpful. The purpose is to ensure we do not create groups entirely of quiet students who are not likely to talk, or groups of students who all struggle with collaboration, and that groups are balanced. This organization process is just the first step in determining the makeup of groups.

Identifying Skills

Although organizing names under behavioral headings is important, we also have to consider skills when creating groups. As the year progresses, you will develop an idea of students' skills based on observation as well as assessments. However, this is nearly impossible at the beginning of the year before you know your students.

To help with this, have students take a skills assessment in the first weeks of the school year. The skills assessment has the simple purpose of identifying how comfortable students feel using certain skills. These skills should include the broad essential skills (collaboration, communication, creativity, time management) as well as specific skills that they will need to complete work in your classroom (video editing, internet searching, writing). This is a self-assessment, so like every other assessment, it should be used as a guide to gauge their understanding, not the rule. Collecting data about how adept students believe they are at certain skills is an effective way to create groups before you have a deeper understanding of their abilities.

Here is an example of a skills assessment:

For each statement, there will be three answers for you to choose from:

1. This statement does not apply to me at all.
2. This statement sometimes applies to me.
3. This statement always applies to me.

Essential Skills

1. I enjoy presenting in front of people.
2. I work better when I am working with other people.
3. I am an artist.
4. When I can't do something, I give up quickly.
5. I like leading groups.
6. I share during class discussions.
7. When I have a problem with somebody, I let them know it.
8. I am a hard worker.
9. I pay attention to detail in my work.

Technical Skills

1. I am comfortable using new technologies.
2. I have experience video editing.
3. If I don't know something, I can find the answer on the internet.
4. I like solving problems using math.
5. I like to communicate my ideas in writing.
6. I like when I get to read.

Get the Skills Assessment in the Collaborative Classroom Toolkit at trevormuir.com/resources.

This skills assessment should be tailored to your class and the type of tasks your students accomplish. When you have this information, you can then use it to create groups. If my students are completing a task that has a video component, I want to make sure each group has someone who identified that they are comfortable with video skills or at least with using new technologies. If it's the beginning of the year and I have not identified the students in my class who are prone to leadership, I can take the information from the skills assessment and place a self-identified leader in each group.

It's important to spread skills out so that each group can be balanced and benefit from what everyone brings to the table. You don't want one group full of "big thinker" students who do not pay attention to detail, and another that is made up entirely of detail-oriented students. Effective collaboration is based on balance; the skills assessment can help give some directions toward that balance at the beginning of the year.

Researchers for the *Harvard Business Review*[2] discovered that the more experts on a given subject a team has, the more likely that team is to be nonproductive. Essentially, groups thrive when there is diversity. This can mean skills diversity, which means having students who possess different skill sets in each group. It also means racial, socioeconomic, and gender diversity. Homogeneity is limiting. There's less vibrance; it lacks alternative thinking and ways to solve problems. Researcher Lynda Gratton says, "Input and expertise of people with disparate views and backgrounds creates cross-fertilization that sparks insight and innovation."[2]

This is where knowing your students' skills and preferences can spark innovation in a collaborative classroom.

I have to make this clear: this is not an exact science. Throughout the year, as students develop new skills or realize they possess traits that they did not know they had, you can shift groups accordingly. New leaders will emerge; quiet kids will learn to discuss; uninspired students will learn the value of hard work. This will obviously have an impact on how you choose groups.

When students begin to thrive with new people in different settings, hopefully they will see the value of group assignments. They will learn that they are capable of working with people they are not yet close with and may discover that they can even succeed with people they do not like. When their teacher chooses groups with intentionality and purpose, they are equipping students with capabilities they will use throughout their lives as they enter college groups and workplaces where they will have little say about who they collaborate with. And hopefully, because of this, students will not think you are a crotchety old teacher bent on using your power to make their lives miserable by not letting them sit with their friends.

Reflection

1. What is most important to consider when creating groups?
2. How does the information on optimal group size affect how you and your peers collaborate?
3. How can you embrace diversity (racial, socioeconomic, gender, etc.) more in your classroom?

CHAPTER 7

LEARNING TO GIVE AND RECEIVE CONSTRUCTIVE CRITICISM

We now have a workforce full of people who need constant reassurance and can't take criticism. Not a recipe for success in business, where taking on challenges, showing persistence, and admitting and correcting mistakes are essential.

—Carol S. Dweck, *Mindset*

In 2009 a top-secret team of tech engineers at Google began work on a project with the aim of revolutionizing the world. Only a few years after the release of the iPhone, a supercomputer that fits in your pocket, the top scientists and researchers at Google set their sights on an innovation that would usurp even the mightiest competition. Rather than keeping that phone/camera/computer/GPS/game console/etc. in your pocket, this top-secret team would enable you to wear it on your face.

This team was developing what would eventually be called Google Glass, a pair of glasses that would bring your smartphone directly to your field of vision. Google envisioned Glass to be a fashion statement, a tech tool, and a hands-free means to stay connected in a way previously only dreamed of in science fiction. Google Glass would be one of those inventions that would change the way humans interacted in the world.

The internal fervor for this innovation grew so quickly that the team at Google decided they could not stay top-secret anymore. Google co-founder Sergey Brin had the idea of releasing Google Glass to a section of the public during its testing phase, getting critiques and making iterations externally rather than from within. Glass was released with unbelievable fanfare, and the sleek glasses were tried on by presidents, kings, fashion models, and of course, Oprah. *Time Magazine* named it one of the "best inventions of the year,"[1] and by all estimations, Google Glass was set to revolutionize the way we use technology.

But users started wearing them in bathrooms, and people grew very uncomfortable with standing next to someone at a urinal who could very well be recording a video. Casinos all over Las Vegas began banning them to prevent cheating. Film studios grew concerned about piracy, and movie theaters banned them nationwide. There were mass complaints about terrible battery life on the Glass, distracted driving, and the health concern of having a cell phone attached to your head all day, as well as the public being unclear of its primary purpose. People didn't know what they were supposed to do with it!

In January of 2015, on the same day *Inc. Magazine*[2] named Google Glass "the worst tech gadget ever invented," Google discontinued all sales of Google Glass. The project was dead, contributing to a 3.6 billion-dollar loss for Google that same year.

This all begs the question, did Google Glass fail simply because of a poor product, or because Google released a product that was not yet ready? Rather than spending the time to critique and revise this ambitious innovation amongst the team of designers and engineers, Google slapped Glass with a $1,500 price tag and released it to the public. It wasn't scrutinized and tested the way it should have been, and as a result, it was a colossal failure.

Constructive Feedback Is Essential

It's so easy to become overzealous about something you have poured your time and energy into, overlooking key details that can be spotted with strong critical feedback. This can sometimes lead to epic failures such as Google Glass. It also can mean presenting a creation that is incomplete, not having reached its full potential. It can be the difference between good and great. What you created might be serviceable or you might do well on a task, but was it excellent? Were you superb?

Excellence happens when we open ourselves up to critique, allowing others to give their perspectives and feedback, and being willing to use that feedback to improve. This is difficult to do because the work that we do is personal, and it can be extremely difficult to separate critical feedback from our work and ourselves. Closing ourselves and our work off from constructive criticism creates a one-dimensional echo chamber and inhibits growth progress.

If we want students to grow and strive for excellence, they have to become aware of the importance of getting this feedback on their work, and they also have to be taught how to give it. Constructive feedback plays a critical role in collaboration because it helps ensure that whatever groups are working on actually succeeds. Too many of my students in the past thought that whatever they were creating was strong, only to be surprised in the end that it wasn't. Either the feedback was all positive and there was not enough honesty, or there were no opportunities for feedback at all.

One time my students listened to a former refugee from a developing country tell her story of traveling to America and not knowing how to use many of the technologies we take for granted in our highly modernized world. After hearing her story and feeling compelled to act on it, my students decided to create tools to help incoming refugees better assimilate into our society. Along with this, they learned history and English content, the subject matter of the class that aligns with this issue.

One of the problems the guest speaker shared was not knowing what kind of food to buy at the grocery store. Therefore, one of my groups had the idea of making a cookbook that would be translated into the different languages of refugees. I heard their basic idea, said it was great, and let the group work. At the end of the project, they presented it to a panel of social workers who aid refugees. The students were hoping the tools that they created would be accepted by the agency and actually used to serve refugees in our community. Talk about a real-world project!

The cookbook group presented their project and showed off their recipes to the panel. The recipes included items such as Crème Brûlée, braised pork, and grilled mahi-mahi. (Apparently one of my students had just returned from a vacation in Hawaii.)

After the students' presentation to the panel, a member of the panel said something along the lines of, "That's a beautiful cookbook, it really is. But those recipes are really not what the clients we serve are looking for. They need recipes for basic meals, like hotdogs and mac-and-cheese." And in kind but direct words, the social worker said, "Thanks for your work, but we will not be using your product in our program."

Ouch.

The group was disappointed. They were passionate about their idea and worked hard on creating the final product. However, they failed to consider who they were serving and what need they were meeting. They didn't ask each other the hard questions. The group did not critique their idea before diving into the bulk of the work. Someone came up with an idea, everyone got excited about it, and the whole group dove headfirst into making it a reality. They had pulled a Google Glass.

As a teacher, this group's failure (which was a learning moment for them) was a realization for me of how important constructive feedback is throughout *all stages of a project*. Up until this point, I would provide feedback on their work at the end of a project, and for this one specifically, I intended for students to get feedback from the professional audience, the social work panel. However, at this point it was too late for the feedback to be meaningful. Students could not act on the criticism they were given. As a result, their work suffered and was not chosen to be used by the agency.

The process of giving and receiving constructive criticism must be woven into the entirety of the work we do. The creative process requires iterations to achieve the best possible outcomes. When I write a book, maybe 70 percent of the time is spent actually writing it, and the other 30 percent is spent responding to feedback from friends and editors who read each draft. I shudder to think what you would think of me as a writer if you only read my first draft!

Students need to know how to constantly vet an idea and its creation if they want it to succeed, and it's up to the teacher to show them how to do that.

The Tuning Protocol

The tuning protocol is a process from the Project-Based Learning framework that can be used in many different facets of a learning environment. The purpose of this protocol is to give a structure to provide strong critical feedback. The protocol looks like this:

1. In the first step, group members present an idea or something they are creating to an audience. The audience can be the rest of the class or other small groups.
   a. The presenters present for an allotted amount of time (two to three minutes).
   b. During the presentation, audience members silently record everything they *like* about the idea or product, as well as everything they *wonder* about what can be done to improve it.
2. In the second step, after the presentation, audience members have a discussion together, sharing their "likes and wonders."
   a. While the audience discusses, the presenters should listen and record everything that they hear.
   b. The presenters are not allowed to respond to the feedback during the second step but can only listen to the conversation. Their focus should be solely on listening to feedback and not on responding to it. You might even find it helpful to have the presenters turn and face away from the audience as they listen and record feedback.

After tuning, the presenting group now has a list of aspects of their idea or project that were well received, and they have a list of criticisms they might need to take into consideration. Notice how

I said "*might* need," because not all critical feedback is necessarily merited or useful. The presenters might hear something that they decide collectively they do not want to use, and that is fine. However, they still need to write it down when they hear it, because part of the exercise is learning how to listen to all feedback.

Description, Not Judgment

When students are first introduced to tuning, the process can be uncomfortable to them. They might not want to offend their peers with any type of criticism of their project, and often they heap on praise and give presenters a huge list of likes and not enough wonders. This is why it is so crucial for the teacher to model how to give feedback. Create a list yourself of all the wonders you have, and if students do not say them first, share them with the class. Stress to students that you are not in any way criticizing their abilities; you are helping improve their work so that it can be excellent.

We have to make it clear to students that as long as the feedback is constructive and about the product and not the person, then it should be encouraged. Only sharing what you like and saying something is perfect is dishonest and counterproductive. The whole point of the protocol is to weed out anything that is hindering the project from succeeding and giving suggestions to make it stronger. By only being "nice" you are not helping your peers, which is really not nice at all. In his book *How to Kill a Unicorn*,[3] innovation consultant Mark Payne says, "Ideas are treated not as precious pearls to be polished, but as sparks born of friction [because] exposing fledgling innovation ideas to the tough love of tough questions … ensures those ideas can survive."[3]

Using Productive Language

To take some of the edge off constructive criticism and make it more digestible for students, be strict about the use of the tuning language. Use language that is descriptive and not judgmental. Feedback should describe what is noticed about an idea or project but should not be evaluating whether it is "right or wrong" or "good or bad." Instead of "I don't like that song choice," say, "I wonder whether that song choice is too upbeat for the video." By describing what is noticed rather than judging it, it reduces the need for the recipient of the feedback to be defensive of the right or wrong decision they made.

If critical feedback is being given to a person's performance, give feedback on the behavior rather than the person. Instead of "Alex is a good speaker," the feedback should be something like, "I like how Alex made eye contact with the audience and spoke clearly." The purpose of the feedback is not to pay a compliment; it's to reinforce what was done well or suggest what can be improved.

Another way to disarm defensiveness to feedback is to require that students start feedback with either "I Like" or "I Wonder." If feedback starts with "They need to" or "You should," the presenting group will immediately be put on the defensive. It sounds like they are being given a command, and people naturally resist commands from peers. However, when feedback sounds like this: "I wonder if Crème Brûlée is a recipe refugees need right when they get to America," then it is a suggestion for the group to consider addressing.

This language is helpful during tuning but is also the strong primary language for any type of healthy criticism. When my five-year-old son is considering throwing a baseball in the same room as our television, I say to him, "I wonder if that is the best idea?" I'm implying what decision I want him to make, and with my five-year-old, very close to demanding it, but I leave him the element of choice. He is forced to think about his decision and what will result from it. Simply telling him what to do in that situation, especially if he's anything like me, will make him want to throw the ball even more.

Encouraging More Likes Than Wonders

Critical feedback is not an indictment on the person, but rather suggestions to improve that person's work. For it to be well received, the whole process should be a positive one. If all a student is hearing is what is wrong with their work and the positives are not highlighted enough, that student can feel overwhelmed and resigned to not making the necessary improvements.

Researchers Emily Heaphy and Marcial Losada conducted a study[4] for *The American Behavioral Scientist* measuring the effectiveness of positive and negative feedback in a business setting. After analyzing sixty different collaborative teams within a large information-processing company, they found that there is value in both positive and constructive feedback, but the proportion of the feedback is what is crucial. The highest achieving teams used five times as much positive feedback as negative. The lowest achieving teams used a much smaller ratio of negative to positive feedback.

The truth is, people respond better to positivity. The likes get the presenter's attention and adjust their mindset so that when they do get the constructive feedback, it can be well-received. This isn't about inflating students' egos and telling them untrue positives about their work, but it does mean paying close attention to anything that stands out as effective, and communicating that first.

Applying Tuning outside of the Protocol

This also means explaining to students why constructive criticism is important. You don't require that students give likes before wonders simply because it's a rule. You do this because you know the value of positivity, and students need to understand this value. Like everything else in a collaborative classroom, students should know why they are doing what they do. Some of this might sound intuitive, but it is not the cultural norm. In far too many educational settings, students are used to receiving feedback on their work after it is completed, and often this feedback is a grade that cannot be changed. Few opportunities are given to make iterations, and if the grade is negative, so is the feedback and the student's response to it.

A language shift has to occur. Using the tuning protocol, whether it's to improve ideas, products, presentations, or even writing assignments, there is a great way to teach this skill. The skill must be transferable beyond the protocol. Students should be encouraged to use "like and wonder" language outside of the structured setting.

"How does my poster look?"

"Ooh, I like the colors you chose. I like how that font is modern looking. I like that you chose to use illustrations. I wonder if that heading is big enough for people to clearly read?"

Students don't need their teacher present to have this type of interaction. They just have to know the value of using this language. They need to see why starting with positive comments first is more beneficial than starting with negative ones. Students have to have experience viewing something with a critical eye so that their feedback can be productive.

Above all else, they need to see the value of asking for this type of feedback and know how to respond to it. It will bolster their work and help them achieve excellence. Collaboration will become about more than just working together; it will become about strengthening each other.

Critical feedback will also go a long way to prevent wearable smartphones from ever becoming a thing.

Reflection

1. How does it feel for you to receive constructive criticism?
2. What factors have kept you from giving constructive criticism to your peers?
3. What does it mean to *describe* rather than *judge*?
4. How does language play a role in how criticism is given and received?

Take Action

Plan to use the tuning protocol in a specific upcoming activity in your classroom.

#CollaborativeClassroom

CHAPTER 8

THE ART OF CLASS DISCUSSIONS

You must be able to say "I understand,"
before you can say any one of the
following things: "I agree," or
"I disagree," or "I suspend judgment."

—Mortimer J. Adler, *How to Read a Book*

When I first joined Twitter in 2010, each time I logged on was like sitting down in a virtual meeting room with dynamic educators spread across the globe. A teacher from Arizona would tweet about promoting creativity in schools, I'd respond from my couch in Michigan, and for the next hour, teachers from around the world would discuss why or why not schools needed more creativity. People would tweet blog articles they wrote relating to the discussion, cite research, tell stories, sometimes argue, and at the end of these discussions I would log off Twitter with a swollen brain after engaging in a discussion that would directly impact the work I did in school the next day.

In 2010, Twitter was a breeding ground for rich discussion and conversations.

Flash forward a decade. This morning I saw on Twitter thousands of replies to a negative comment about Ariana Grande's hairstyle, thousands of others agreeing or disagreeing with an insult the American president tweeted, and of course, endless inspirational tweets designed to get as many likes and retweets as possible.

Couple this with Pew Research Center data[1] that shows that 95 percent of people, including teenagers, have access to a smartphone, and 45 percent of teens say they are connected to the internet on a near-constant basis. This tool that has a dominant tendency to weaken public discourse is constantly at everyone's fingertips, and as a result, public discourse seems to be eroding.

Before I get too doom-and-gloomy, I should state that there are still many fruitful connections happening all over Twitter and the internet. It's not all political arguments where no one is listening to anyone, debates about pop star hair-care products, and quotes that belong on bumper stickers. Yet, it's not difficult to notice the major trend in how people discuss online. The accessibility and anonymity of the internet has made it a place people go to share opinions without gaining new ones. Online discussions are often about proving points rather than hearing diverse points of view. Hiding behind a screen and keyboard makes people feel invincible; mean words and false information go unchecked and have little if any ramification as soon as the app is closed. And the apps are increasingly being closed less and less.

One of the major ramifications of this is that how people talk to each other online has a direct impact on how they discuss, or don't discuss, in real life. This has an impact on many aspects of a person's life, including their professional life. Jeff Weiner, the CEO of LinkedIn, says, "Communications is the number one skills gap [for employees]."[2] The ability to listen and respond to others is critical in the modern workforce. Whether working in a traditionally communicative job such as sales or business leadership, or in a technical field and even in accounting, people have to be able to discuss. Communication is essential for healthy collaboration now more than ever, making the erosion of discussion skills so pertinent.

That's it for the doom-and-gloom, because now I've got great news: people can *learn* how to discuss! Discussion skills can be re-strengthened and taught. This is why discussion is one of the key pillars in a collaborative classroom. In fact, there should never be a single day in the school year in which students are not conversing with each other and given some type of opportunity to discuss. Whether the discussion is academic or social, students need to develop the ability to communicate effectively, and teachers can be very intentional about making that happen.

Components of Healthy Discussion

For students to participate in rich class discussions, the discussions must fit the following criteria:

1. The discussion is safe.

2. The discussion has a clear purpose.
3. The discussion is owned by the students.

Make Discussion Safe

Students, and I mean kindergarten to PhD students, will not engage in class discussion if they feel they will be attacked for expressing their views. No matter what a student says aloud during a discussion, the teacher has to ensure the environment is safe for them to do so.

This sounds easy enough; just don't laugh at or shame a student and the environment will be safe, right? However, even minor incidents can be enough to send a message to students that the class is not safe to discuss, and as a result class discussion will become a place where students are afraid to dive in and contribute beyond the surface level.

One time my class was having a whole-group discussion about a novel we were reading. One boy kept raising his hand to talk, and when I called on him for the fourth time, I blurted out, "Okay, we've heard enough from you on this! Let's hear someone else." As soon as the words left my mouth, I realized they were the wrong ones.

Immediately that student put his hand down, feeling slightly shamed, and I could feel the energy drain from the room. No one else wanted to contribute to the discussion, because they believed they could be called out next. I should have said something like, "I'm loving what you have to say, but I want to hear what everyone else thinks as well." Unfortunately, that's not what I said, and I had to rebuild some of the culture in the class to get students to discuss again.

Speaking up in class takes courage, especially when it is a new skill. We have to create an environment that doesn't impede this skill.

Along with monitoring yourself, this also means facilitating class discussion to ensure that other students keep it safe as well. This is why it's beneficial to have discussion ground rules that are on display and reviewed before every discussion. These rules can be something that you develop with your class, asking them what guidelines should be followed during class discussion. Here's an example of what the ground rules can look like:

Collaborative Classroom Discussion Ground Rules

1. Listen respectfully when someone else is talking.
2. Be critical of ideas, not people.
3. Allow everyone a chance to speak.
4. Ask for clarification if you are confused.
5. Always work toward a shared understanding.
6. Collaborate, don't compete.
7. If you are offended by something, call it out immediately.

 Get the Classroom Discussion Ground Rules Poster in the Collaborative Classroom Toolkit at trevormuir.com/resources.

The ground rules are non-negotiable, for yourself and for students. Part of your role in facilitating discussion is ensuring that they are followed by the students, and that you also follow them to keep the discussion environment safe for everyone.

Purposeful Discussions

Authenticity is at the heart of student engagement. When students engage in work that matters to them and they see its benefit, they will be much more likely to immerse themselves in the work. To maximize discussions with your class, you have to find ways to make them authentic. This starts with "stating the why."

Try to make apparent before any type of discussion why the class is having it. If your students just finished reading a passage and you are about to have them turn and talk about it, first say, "*I want you to hear what the people around you thought about the reading to see how it compares with or is different from what you thought,* so turn and talk to your neighbor about it."

This simple line is giving purpose to the discussion. They are not discussing with partners because that is just what they do in your class; they're doing it for a specific reason.

The purpose also has to be relevant to students for it to be a motivating factor. Students value their schoolwork more when that work is relevant to their own lives. Researchers David Yeager and Angela Duckworth conducted a study in which high-poverty high school seniors took an online multiple choice test containing "boring math problems."[3] Next to the math problems were links to viral YouTube videos students could click and watch at any time rather than complete the problems. The students were told they would not be penalized for watching the videos if they chose to.

One set of seniors took the test without any prepping, and unsurprisingly, many watched the videos and did poorly on the math test. However, another group, before taking the test, were told that the practice from this test would benefit them in college. They were shown scientific studies that proved the value of this kind of math and how it would help them in their future careers.

This group of students did far better on the test than the first group. The students were from the same schools and had the same teachers, but those who were motivated with relevance and authenticity outperformed the other group.

This is why discussion in the classroom must have purpose, and that purpose should be apparent to students. When creating a lesson plan that has a discussion in it, spend a few extra minutes thinking about the purpose of the discussion, and devise a plan for how you will explain that purpose to students. Include why it's important for the task at hand, which is understanding the content, but also explain the transcendent purpose of the discussion. Why does this matter to them? Why is the hard work of deep discussions worth having in class, when it would be much easier to sit it out and not say anything?

Beyond the explanation, find ways to make discussions personal in some way. If you are going to have a discussion on the Declaration of Independence, start by asking the question, "When was a time in your life that you wanted to rebel?" This serves as a hook, grabbing students' attention with personal relevance before diving deeper into the content.

Sixty-nine percent of teachers reported that their students were not interested in learning.[4] Ideally, creating a more engaging curriculum and having more captivating discussions would solve this problem. Although we should always strive to make curriculum more engaging and that does raise student interest in the classroom, coursework is not (and doesn't have to be) interesting all the time. We are doing our students a disservice if we only expect them to work hard and contribute when they are not bored. Far too much of life is boring at times to frame the classroom as an unrealistic place that never has dull moments. Students must learn how to work hard when the subject matter does not interest them.

This is where the value of a higher-level purpose comes in. Whether it's a full-class discussion or students talking to a partner for thirty seconds, having purpose for the discussion will amplify engagement no matter the task.

Make Discussion Student-Owned

I remember a time in one of my classes of freshmen, which by the way was one of the most difficult groups of students I'd ever taught, when I was holding a discussion on gender inequality. I stood in the front of the room, and students faced me as I called on raised hands to contribute to the discussion. Only a couple of students, unfortunately, dared to put their hands up for such a contentious topic. After the class heard the same two students give their opinions for what seemed like ten times each, the discussion stalled, and I could hear nothing but crickets in my classroom.

This was an incredibly important discussion to have, and one that was extremely relevant to my students, but getting most of them to say a word about it was like getting fifteen-year-olds to not look at their phones for an hour. I halted the discussion for the day and told students we'd return to it tomorrow.

The next day at the beginning of class, I had students write down all of the ways they saw gender inequality in their lives. I had them write questions about the topic that could not be answered with *yes* or *no*. After they finished writing, they sat in a circle, and I asked them to have a discussion with everything they just wrote. At first there was silence as they waited for me to ask the first discussion question, and I just responded that I was going to sit this one out, and they could lead. There was an awkward silence as they looked down at their writing and questions, and finally one brave girl said, "I don't think it's fair girls have dress code restrictions and boys don't. What do you guys think?"

All of a sudden, it seemed every student in the room tried to chime in at once with their opinion, many agreeing and disagreeing, and for the rest of class these students sat around and talked about gender inequality. The next day the students came into my room begging to have another discussion. That is not hyperbole, they were literally pleading to sit in a circle and discuss. For the rest of that school year, this class of students that was so difficult to manage had a new culture built on having discussions.

Part of their engagement was attributable to the relevance of the discussions. They liked talking about things that mattered to them. However, the discussions were also rich when we talked about an act from Shakespeare or using tone in poetry. On the day we discussed gender inequality, I discovered the value of student ownership in discussions. When students have control of their work and guide it in the direction they want, they will be much more deeply invested than if the teacher is in complete control. Research published in the *Journal of Educational Psychology*[4] shows that students are more engaged and even develop a deeper understanding of the material when they have ownership of it.

This makes sense. Is there anything worse as a teacher than having to use scripted curriculum, being told what to teach, how to teach, and even when to teach it? We are more passionate and more empowered when we are trusted with our classrooms and to lead them as we see fit. Now, it's still helpful to receive leadership and guidance to lead our classes, but everyone wants to have ownership of their work and be trusted as professionals.

The same is true for students. Student empowerment is one of the most powerful teaching tools imaginable. It's also one of the most difficult ones to use. For one, the traditional model of education is extremely teacher-centered. The teacher plans. The teacher dictates. The teacher leads. This is how most of us knew school, and it is not easy to shift that paradigm.

It's also not easy to give away control. Student-led activities, especially discussion, can be messy work. Teachers can plan the activities leading up to discussion, but if it is truly student-led, it will be full of unknowns as soon as it begins. This raises questions about how effective the discussion will be. Will it hit the benchmarks and targets that have to be met? Will the discussion stay on track or veer off as discussions often do?

These are realistic concerns and are often what prevents teachers from giving away control of discussions. It's vital that teachers become facilitators rather than leaders of discussions, for the sake of strong collaboration, student engagement, and deeper learning.

One of the best ways to do this is to use specific strategies that promote student ownership. Here are a few examples:

Samoan Circle

The Samoan Circle is a fast-paced strategy designed to facilitate large group discussion and allow participants to share and listen to each other's points of view. It's especially helpful for conflict resolution or to discuss a controversial topic, but it can really be used for any discussion topic.

To hold a Samoan Circle, place four chairs in the middle of your classroom and have the entire class form a circle around them. The class will have a discussion, but students can only speak if they are sitting in one of the four chairs in the middle. Everyone outside of the chairs must listen. If a student wants to join the discussion, they can tap a student's shoulder sitting in a chair, and as soon as that student is finished speaking, they must vacate the chair and let in the newcomer. The discussion is really not about those sitting in the chairs, but for the entire group involved. The room is silent except for four students in the middle of the circle, and the discussion can move with the rhythm of students revolving in and out.

Every time I do a Samoan Circle, I see students wriggle in their silent impatience to get into one of the chairs and share their thoughts, engaging in the content of the discussion by listening more than talking. Students control the pace and direction of the discussion while the teacher stands on the outside, facilitating only when necessary.

Conver-Stations

This is a wonderful idea from teacher Sarah Brown Wessling. For this strategy, put students in groups of four to six and give each group a question to discuss. As mentioned previously, students can generate these questions before the activity. After they have discussed for several minutes, or however long it takes for the discussion to develop, two members from each group should rotate to a different group, and everyone else remains.

Once students have rotated, the discussion continues, and the new arrivals are brought into it, contributing what they talked about at their previous group. These rotations can continue as many times as you see fit, as each one freshens the conversations and new students bring new and different ideas. Students have complete ownership of the discussion, and teachers can roam around the room listening and contributing to different groups however they'd like.

Another benefit to Conver-Stations is that students are constantly getting to move, which prevents the discussion from becoming stagnant. Additionally, students are having to synthesize their discussions each time they move, which gives them a deeper understanding of the content.

Harkness Discussion

The Harkness discussion method, developed by the Phillip Exeter Academy, is the epitome of student-owned discussion. It is a learning model based entirely around students listening to and speaking with each other. Students are given a topic or piece of content to explore and discover individually or in small groups. Along with this new knowledge, students should prepare questions they have for each other about it. Then they are put into a circle to discuss the content. The goal is for everyone to contribute to the discussion, asking questions and responding to each other, and participation can even be graded based on how students contribute.

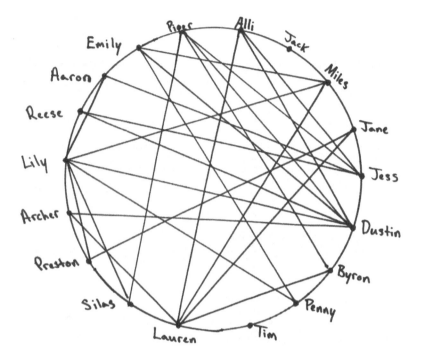

The teacher's role is only to help the discussion move between topics, correct inaccurate information, or probe for more detail. Otherwise, they are removed from the circle and are merely observers tracking the flow of the discussion. One way to do this is to create a discussion diagram. Draw a circle on a piece of paper, and place dots on the outside of the circle representing each student. Each time a new student speaks, draw a line from the previous speaker to that dot. By the end of the discussion, the diagram will reveal who contributed and who did not, but also how many times certain students spoke.

After each Harkness discussion, show the diagram to students so they can see the flow of conversation. Have a separate discussion about it, taking note of who spoke to whom and why. Observe patterns such as students addressing people primarily across the room or only people directly next to them. Talk about how to improve discussion next time and increase its value. You can talk to individual students with the diagram, and encourage them to speak more next time, or for more talkative students, to give others the chance to speak.

When first introducing Harkness to students, the discussion can be filled with moments of silence, because most students are not used to being in charge of class discussions. This silence is awkward, and students will be uncomfortable and naturally try to fill it. This is usually prompted by the students who are more inclined to talk, and others will follow suit the more you do it, especially when participation is stressed. They'll also learn that coming to a Harkness discussion unprepared will lead to more of the awkwardness and stagnant conversation.

Part of the value of Harkness is the silence. As a teacher, don't interject or try to fill the silent moments. Let these gaps be times when students think and reflect so that when they do contribute, it will be richer and more thought-provoking. This will transfer to the discussions that students have outside of the class and throughout life.

Model Healthy Discussions

For students to learn how to engage in healthy discussion, they need to see what this looks like first. Set aside time early in the school year for you to have a discussion with other professionals in front of your class. The purpose of this model discussion is for students to see what unhealthy and healthy discussion looks like.

Have your class sit in a circle and place chairs in the center. Invite another teacher, administrator, staff member, parent, or even friend to your class to have a discussion. It could be multiple people or just one other person. Choose a topic everyone can speak about and tell students that you brought this person/people in to have a conversation and that they are invited to listen in.

For the first part of the discussion, intentionally do everything wrong. Talk out of turn, do not listen to other people's words, make no eye contact, pull out your cell phone when they are mid-sentence; don't respond when it is clear that you are supposed to. Be blatant about making it a horrible discussion. Students will most likely laugh as they see their teacher be intentionally rude and disrespectful to the guest. That is the point!

When you can't act anymore and you've made your point, pause and reflect with your students. Ask questions such as:

- What are some things I did poorly in the discussion?
- How did the people I was discussing with respond?
- How does it make you feel to watch that?
- What do you think I learned during the discussion?

After reflecting, it's time to have a healthy discussion. Make strong eye contact, listen intently, share your perspective in a clear and concise way; respectfully disagree with others. After this step, reflect again with students on why this was a better discussion.

As simple as this sounds, modeling discussion is one of the most beneficial things you can do for students in teaching them discussion skills. Many students will not have seen it elsewhere. It's rarely found in media, and much of school is spent sitting quietly or sharing aloud to an entire class. Every single year, I can reference back to the model discussion and ask students for that type of discussion in small groups or with the whole class. It is a powerful, yet simple way to instill this important skill.

Class Debates

I know the discussion ground rules say not to compete, so maybe this belongs in another section, but class debates are an excellent way to get competitive students invested in sharing aloud in class. I have seen many quiet students fall in love with debating, and their skills and confidence carry over to discussions.

Debates are a way for students to learn how to respectfully disagree with someone while trying to prove a point using different methods of persuasion. The goal of any classroom debate is to persuade an audience to agree with a certain point of view or perspective within a structured format. By arguing in a rigid format and only speaking at certain times while following a set of rules for debate, students learn to listen and react to each other. Students are also learning how to support their thoughts and opinions with evidence, and how to communicate the evidence in a persuasive way.

Part of what makes discussion rich is that participants in it are informed. Having students prepare for a debate models how to become knowledgeable on a certain subject. This makes them better debaters, which is useful if they ever become politicians, but more importantly, it instills in students these skills for use outside of the structured format.

To teach students debate, start with something small and inconsequential. Put the class into groups and hold debates about whether PlayStation or XBOX is better, or Batman vs Superman, or Chevy vs Ford, or dogs vs cats, or should schools have uniforms, or should schools ban tag at recess, or whatever else can be debated. Whatever you choose, the debate is something fun and easy to practice with. However, although the topic is light, have a rigid debate structure that the class will follow. Require that students may not talk while the other team has the floor and discuss other debate etiquette. The format could look something like this:

Debate Format

1. INTRODUCTION (2 minutes)

   Team A

   Team B

2. OPPOSITION (2 minutes)

   Team A

3. REBUTTAL (1 minute)

   Team B

4. OPPOSITION (2 minutes)

   Team B

5. REBUTTAL (1 minute)

   Team A

6. CLOSING (45 seconds)

   Team B

   Team A

While the two teams are debating, have the rest of the class evaluate them for these criteria:

- Every judge should fill out a DEBATE VOTING FORM for each team in the debate.
- You may not have any biases when voting for debaters
- 0 = missing; 1 = weak; 2 = developing; 3 = adequate; 4 = strong

1. Opening statements were clear, introduced your historical figure, and addressed the central issues of the debate.

       0   1   2   3   4

2. Opposition effectively points out flaws in opposing leader.

       0   1   2   3   4

3. Rebuttal statements effectively addressed the opposition.

       0   1   2   3   4

4. Final statements effectively summarized the team's main points and improved the team's position.

        0   1   2   3   4

5. Claims show evidence of research AND reasoning.

        0   1   2   3   4

6. Overall impression of the presentation—eye contact, use of voice, use of appeals, **all** group members participated.

        0   1   2   3   4

7. Participants adhered to rules and procedures (followed debate etiquette).

        0   1   2   3   4

8. Is there any essential information that was left out of the debate or was inaccurate? If so, please explain the information that the team missed. (Facilitators may deduct up to 10 points from the group's score for invalid or missed information.)

Possible Total: 28

By having students score the debates, they are intentionally looking for proper debate etiquette and understanding what it takes to win structured arguments. Once students understand this process, debates can be used throughout the year as a strategy to deepen content understanding.

In any class in which there are at least two sides to an issue, you can use the debate format to teach and reinforce the content. In a Language Arts class, students can debate the meaning of a novel; in science class they could answer the question: "Should the government ban fossil fuels?"; in history class, debate the justification of a certain war—or whatever else fits your content area that has more than one side to it. To debate, students have to research, craft arguments and counterarguments, and practice their presentations. These are all activities that cause them to go beyond the surface level of understanding. Students are building deeper understanding of content, but they also are fostering lifelong skills.

Teaching Students to Listen

One of the most difficult aspects of discussion is not the speaking part. It's not conveying your thoughts in a clear and concise way or even gathering all of the knowledge and information to share.

It's listening.

Actively hearing what someone else is saying is a skill in its own right. It's so tempting during a discussion to pretend you are listening to your peers, when in reality you are just planning what you are going to say next. I think about those staff meetings in which I sit in a room with faculty discussing a certain topic, gearing up to raise my hand and share my thoughts on the matter. I rehearse in my head what I'm going to say. I'm organizing all of the thoughts I have on the topic and figuring out how I'm going to make my point clearly, but also not sound bossy, and also not sound whiny, and also not sound like a know-it-all, and also make sure my voice doesn't squeak, and also sound like I'm intelligent and know what I'm talking about.

Someone else, meanwhile, is sharing, and I don't hear a single word they say.

Sound familiar?

Discussions can too often turn into a bunch of people giving individual speeches to no one, negating the entire point of the discussion. This is why it is imperative to teach students to actively listen to each other and be less concerned with how they will sound when they speak, and to be more focused on having a purposeful and rich discussion.

Focus on Listening Posture

Part of active listening is about posture. How students look during discussion, including their orientation, facial expressions, eye contact, and movement, has a huge influence on their engagement. Model proper and improper posture to students during a discussion. Have them point out what they notice.

Then have a class discussion and challenge students to mirror you during it. If they are properly mirroring you, they should all be leaning in when someone is talking, nodding their heads when they comprehend a point, smiling regularly, and maintaining eye contact. Use this mirroring challenge for the next few discussions to reinforce this point. Students will begin to mirror each other in further discussions, using not only their ears but their bodies to listen to what others are saying.

Listening Protocols

Having free and open discussions can be great, and that will be what students have for most of their lives. As they are learning this skill and developing the ability to listen well, it's helpful to have protocols that promote and require listening.

Repeat before Response

For this discussion protocol, students have to paraphrase the main idea of the person who spoke before them before speaking themselves. The first speaker then confirms whether what was repeated was accurate and clarifies anything that was left out. Once the first speaker confirms that the listener understands what was said, the roles reverse, and the listener can share their thoughts and information.

This protocol requires that students hear everything a person says, and therefore they are not able to plan their own responses while the other person is speaking. After the first round, pause and let the first listener think about and formulate their response.

Save the Last Word for Me

This is a protocol developed by Patricia Averette that can be done in small groups and challenges students to listen over a longer period of time. Here is the process:

1. Create a group of four participants. Choose a timekeeper.
2. Each participant silently identifies what they consider to be the most significant idea addressed in an article, video, lecture, etc.
3. When the group is ready, a volunteer member identifies the part of the article (or whatever is being discussed) that they found to be most significant and reads it out loud to the group. This person (the presenter) says nothing about why they chose that particular passage.
4. The group should pause for a moment to consider the passage before moving to the next step.
5. The other three participants each have one minute to respond to the passage—saying what it makes them think about, what questions it raises for them, etc.
6. The first participant then has three minutes to state why they chose that part of the article and to respond to—or build on—what they heard from their colleagues.
7. The same pattern is followed until all four members of the group have had a chance to be the presenter and to have the "last word."
8. Optional: Provide a time for open dialogue about the text and the ideas and questions raised during the first part of the protocol.
9. Debrief the experience.

This is a protocol that requires active listening and is not possible unless all participants are fully engaged in what others are saying.

Timed Discussions

To building listening skills, use a timer during discussions to give structure for when students speak and so that they know when it will be their turn to contribute. Set a timer for two minutes, and during that time, only the speaker may speak. Encourage listeners to not interrupt or even make agreement or disagreement sounds and gestures. Even if the speaker finishes speaking with thirty seconds remaining, everyone should stay silent for the rest of the two minutes. This pause time might be awkward, but students can use it to process what was said before a new speaker. Part of the anxiety that comes from class discussion is students not knowing when they will speak, and therefore their inner voice gets louder instead of quieter, interrupting their discussion. Having a timer gives this structure and can alleviate those fears and the noise that come with them.

Assessing Discussion

Part of students growing in their ability to discuss is to know their progress and how well they are developing this skill. Teachers can use every discussion as an assessment to track progress and use the data to help students improve. If the class is doing a Samoan Circle, the teacher can choose to observe a couple of students while they interact in the discussion. Each time the selected students enter the circle the teacher makes notes on how they contribute, noting strengths and room for growth. These notes can then be shared with the student to discuss what they are doing well and what can be improved the next time they discuss in class.

Having a rubric for discussion can make this process clearer for you and the student. Here's an example of a discussion rubric:

Collaborative Classroom Discussion Rubric

	Exemplary	Effective	Needs Improvement
Preparation	Fully prepared for the discussion. Is knowledgeable of the topic(s) and ready to share knowledge as well as ask thoughtful questions.	Has basic understanding of the topic(s) and shows some evidence of preparation. Has questions to ask but they are mostly surface-level.	Did not come prepared for the discussion. Lacked knowledge of the topic(s) and did not have any prepared questions.
Listening	Intently listens to peers at all times, clearly processing what was said. Responses to others and posture indicate active listening.	Listens to peers most of the time. Most responses and posture reflect active listening during the discussion, but not all of it.	Does not engage in listening. Contributions seem preplanned and are not responses to peers' thoughts and words. Displays poor listening posture.

Speaking	Speaks confidently and was clearly heard and understood by peers. Contributed a number of times to the discussion. Contributions were in-depth and meaningful.	Speaks with confidence but does not always make points clear. Contributed 1 or 2 times. Contributions showed understanding but lacked depth.	Speaks few if any times. Contributions were either off topic, a repetition of someone else's comments, or surface level.
Ground Rules	Follows all of the Discussion Ground Rules.	Follows the Discussion Ground Rules most of the time.	Violates the Discussion Ground Rules a number of times throughout the discussion.

 Get the Classroom Discussion Rubric in the Collaborative Classroom Toolkit at trevormuir.com/resources.

Remember that a rubric is a tool, an indicator to help guide you in guiding students. It is not an exact science, nor is it perfect. This rubric can provide a snapshot for where a student is at a given moment. If a student is having a bad day and is not in the mood to converse, the rubric might not accurately assess their discussion ability. That's why I'm hesitant to enter discussion assessments into the gradebook after a single discussion. When discussion does enter the gradebook, it should reflect a body of work on the student's part (see Chapter 5). Use the rubric numerous times with a student to gauge their competency before making it official with their grades. Always be willing to change the grade as they grow and improve.

The more students have intelligent and challenging discussions, the better they will get at them. The discussion rubric serves to point out how they can get better. A rubric that only serves the gradebook is a massively underutilized tool. It needs to be a conversation starter with students, something you use to discuss how to get better at discussions.

Here's the reality: Your students will probably not sit in many Samoan Circles throughout their lives once they leave school. Rarely will anyone start a timer and require everyone to stay silent while they speak. You may be the last one to ever score their ability to discuss on a rubric. Using the strategies and processes from this chapter is not so that students master these strategies and processes. Instead, it's to help them build their discussion muscles. They will build confidence to be able to share ideas and information instead of leaving them trapped inside their heads. Becoming a better listener in English, math, science, or history class will make them better listeners to their friends, spouses, coworkers, or constituents.

The ability to discuss is not a skill that is all-of-a-sudden needed in the twenty-first century. Informative, healthy, and rich conversations are a part of what it means to be human. They have always been and always will be needed for a thriving society. Whether someone is an introvert or extrovert, Republican or Democrat, accountant or graphic designer, people need to know the art of strong communication. A collaborative classroom is needed to prevent Snapchat, texting, and Twitter from killing the discussion.

Reflection

1. What does having a classroom that is "safe for class discussion" look like?
2. Why do discussions need to have purpose to be fruitful?
3. What are the risks of allowing discussions to be student-owned?
4. What are the benefits?

Take Action

Contact a peer (another teacher, administrator, support staff, etc.) who can join you to model healthy and unhealthy discussion.

#CollaborativeClassroom

CHAPTER 9

WHEN NOT TO COLLABORATE

A boy is a boy. Two boys is half a boy.
And three boys ain't no boy at all.

—Honey Nun

My great-grandparents lived on a huge piece of land in an old brick mansion with no doors, television, or air conditioning on an orange grove in southern Florida. My brothers and I would stay with them for several weeks every summer, learning to "rough it" with our depression-era elders. Every summer we would disconnect from our Nintendos and televisions and basically live in another era. What we wanted to do most on these visits was explore the woods and find adventures on their vast property. But before we could do any of that, we had chores to complete each day. Some days I would be assigned the job of pruning trees with a rusted old saw and hauling the branches to piles to be burned. While I did that, my brothers would get jobs like hauling trash to a garbage pit at the back of the property or picking oranges in the groves to lug back to the house.

As an adult, this hard work in the hot Florida sun formed some of my fondest memories. I learned to work hard and developed calluses on my hands as well as my mind. This work taught me to deal with boredom and monotony and find ways to entertain myself when I was uncomfortable. But I distinctly remember at the time despising this part of our stay at our great-grandparents. My great-grandparents had little sympathy for us kids when we wanted to just play and explore, and there was rarely a day we could get out of the chores.

One evening after a particularly long and hot day, I came up with an idea to make our chores go quicker. I figured if instead of each boy having to do their own task by themselves, which seemed to take forever, we could all do each chore together, the work would thus be completed three times faster. While one person was sawing off limbs, the others could haul the limbs to the brush pile. While one brother picked the oranges, another could catch them in a basket, and the other could carry it back to the house. We could finish our work hours earlier each day and get to spend the rest of our time fishing and swimming and all of the other things we wanted to do in the summer.

I pitched the idea to my great-grandmother, a tough old woman we called Honey Nun, and told her how efficient the work would be from then on. I saw her fight back a smile, and she asked me whether I was sure this would help us get our tasks finished faster. I assured her it would, and she agreed to let us work together the next day. I didn't know why she smiled, but I was excited for the next day and to get our work done before noon.

The next morning, my brothers and I headed out to cut down and haul branches first. Because this was usually my job, I naturally grabbed the saw and told my brothers where to haul the branches. My older brother's response was, naturally, "Wait, why do you get to saw them? I'm stronger and should do that. You haul the branches."

I said, "Because I'm better at it than you. That's why this is always my job."

At this point, a fight ensued, and I ended up storming away from my brothers.

After reconvening, we decided to pick oranges first, because we could all climb the trees and haul the baskets of oranges back together. My little brother climbed to the top of a tree first and started twisting off the oranges to drop into the baskets. As I started to climb, he grabbed a rotten one that was still hanging on the tree and threw it at my head. The soggy orange exploded in my hair and covered me in stinking, rotten, citrus juice. I did what any mature eleven-year-old would do and climbed another tree to grab a rotten orange and threw it back at him. For the next hour, we had an orange fight that ended with us being sticky and smelling. It also ended with the orange baskets sitting empty.

When we got back to the house for lunch, Honey Nun asked whether we were ready to go fishing and swimming. We got excited and said of course! She said, "Great! As long as you are done with all of your tasks, you are free to go."

Our excitement instantly deflated. The orange baskets were still empty, the brush still needed to be hauled, and a mountain of garbage still needed to be brought to the pit. My great-grandma was unrelenting, and she sent us back to work after lunch. Even worse, she wouldn't let us split up and complete our tasks on our own. We had to do each one together the rest of the day.

After hours of fighting and bickering, always complaining that one was working too hard and the others were being lazy, we finally finished our chores. The day was over, and we were spent. As we sat down to dinner with our eighty-five-year-old great-grandparents, Honey Nun explained why she smiled the night before when I asked whether my brothers and I could work together. She told me a saying I will never forget: "A boy is a boy. Two boys is half a boy. And three boys ain't no boy at all."

Collaboration Is Not Always Required

At first glance, one could think my great-grandmother was saying that collaboration should be avoided, that by working together we were actually hampering what could be accomplished. And in this situation, that was true. First, these three brothers were not natural collaborators together. We entered into the collaborative work without a predisposition to working together productively (because we were three fighting, playful, and competitive brothers). However, I don't think her "ain't no boy at all" saying is an admonition on collaboration. She'd lived too long and experienced too much to not see the value of teamwork. Instead, her statement declares a truth that runs counter to so many blog posts, professional developments, and thought leaders: that sometimes collaboration is not necessary.

Every educator has sat in that staff meeting or read that blog post in which they were told to make school more collaborative for students. We are force-fed this idea that it takes "teamwork to make the dream work," and the best results come from a collective effort. And of course this is true so much of the time (that is what this book is about after all), but sometimes we have to be aware of when it's better for students to work independently.

Too often we ask, "How can we get students to collaborate more?" This is the wrong question. This question treats collaboration as a box to check off, and implies that collaboration is the key to a task's success. But collaboration is not the key; it is a tool to achieve success.

Instead we should be asking, "Will collaboration on this project help or hinder?"

Main Course vs Dessert Collaboration

Does the task require collaboration, or is it something that is best done individually? Think of it in terms of a meal. Collaboration should be used when it contributes to the main course, not the dessert. The main course is where you get the calories, vitamins, and sustenance of the meal. The dessert is the unnecessary part. It's nice, often more enjoyable than the main course, but it is not required. It comes after the real eating happens.

We often see this in Project-Based Learning. An educator thinks they are doing true project work, but the project usually happens *after* the learning occurs. For instance, when an English class reads a novel and creates a diorama afterward, the learning came from reading the novel, writing about it, discussing it, etc. The diorama was a dessert at the end—unnecessary, but fun for students. If the diorama never happened, the students still would have learned the same amount.

When projects are mainly desserts, teachers and students soon find them to be a waste of time, because if they are not valuable and necessary, then what's the point? Why should teachers cut out time in the unit for an unnecessary dessert? Why should students want to work at home on something that is really fluff at the end of a project?

This often leads to educators abandoning projects and returning to their old ways of instruction, because ultimately, the new ways are a waste of time.

The same thing happens with collaboration.

Students are asked to collaborate on tasks that would be better done individually. For instance, I once had my students transcribe the audio from one-hour interviews they conducted with World War II veterans. The point of the activity was for them to listen closely to the audio, become more acquainted with the veterans' stories, and then create a written transcript they could work from when writing biographies and creating documentaries.

I made this a collaborative task and told students to listen and transcribe together. It wasn't long before the whole activity unraveled. None of the kids wanted the task of typing, and so time was wasted as groups decided who got that job. Once kids were finally started on the task, students were complaining that they could not hear over the noise of another group's audio. So I asked everyone to use headphones, and it quickly became a task in which one person did all of the work, and the other group members sat around with nothing to do.

The transcription process ended up taking two full days; days that were wasted on a task that should have taken thirty minutes.

As a result, the following year, I had students divide up the audio they needed to transcribe, and each student in every group was responsible for transcribing a specific segment of the interview. They used a shared document, and after thirty minutes, they had full transcripts of hour-long interviews.

This was a task best done individually. The only teamwork required was the accountability that everyone would complete their segment of the transcript. Otherwise, kids worked alone, and the project was more efficient and effective because of it.

Collaboration should be used when necessary, but never to the detriment of the task at hand. More than once, I've learned this from a task failing the first time. Which raises the question: Does a task need to fail to determine the best plan of action?

Short answer: not always.

Extended answer: Every task should be run through a litmus test to determine whether it needs a collaborative effort or whether it is best kept for the individual. If it can pass the test and is determined to *need* group work, excellent. That's another opportunity for students to develop collaborative skills. However, if the assignment is better if completed by individuals, there is no need to force feed collaboration.

To collaborate or not to collaborate, that is the question.

The Litmus Test

A simple formula can help you determine whether a task needs collaboration.

It looks like this:

Desired Outcome–Cost of Collaboration ≥ Individual Effort

The Desired Outcome is the ideal result of a project or assignment. When planning a lesson or unit of instruction, we have to determine what exactly we want the assignment to accomplish. It's goal-setting, or what is known in the teacher-world as TSWs (The Students Will).

The Desired Outcome should include the content knowledge you hope for a student to obtain, as well as the skills you want them to acquire or develop. Determining which content and skills you want students to develop, whether presentation, communication, critical thinking, or creativity skills, is up to the teacher and the standards that have to be covered.

Once the Desired Outcome has been determined, you are essentially asking whether collaboration helps or hinders in this acquisition. Collaboration always carries some type of cost. From the time it takes for group members to acclimate at the beginning of an activity, to filling out group contracts or project management logs, to the inevitable disagreements and tension that can arise during collaboration that always take some amount of time to resolve, collaboration comes at a cost.

Too often we consider this cost and opt for individual tasks. However, despite the cost of collaboration, often the benefits are still worth more than the individual effort.

When building a collaborative culture, it's helpful to work out this formula each time you are weighing whether to give a collaborative assignment. Using a table is great way to do this visually. Write all of the knowledge and skills you hope for students to gain in the first column, the cost of collaboration in the second, and the gains of collaboration in the third.

For example, the table for the documentary transcript assignment could look like this:

Cost of Collaboration Table

Desired Outcomes	Cost of Collaboration	Gains of Collaboration
Understanding of interview subject matter	Time to delegate tasks	Leadership opportunity during delegation process
Listening skills	Project Management Log time	Whole group listens to entire interview
Written transcript of interview	Uneven work distribution among group members	More ears to determine what is said in the audio recording
Attention to detail	Conflict resolution	
	Time for project must be extended by at least double or triple	

 Get the Cost of Collaboration Table in the Collaborative Classroom Toolkit at trevormuir.com/resources.

Once the table is created, you can see whether the gains garnered from collaboration get students closer to the desired outcome. When analyzing this specific table, you could determine that collaboration is probably not worth it. It does not actually help the project achieve success. Yes, it can provide a leadership opportunity to a student in the group who can lead the delegation of tasks, but that was not one of the desired outcomes for the project. Yes, doing the project collaboratively allows the whole group to listen to the interview, but couldn't that be a separate assignment, or even one that students can do on their own time? Will students have other opportunities to understand the subject matter of the interview outside of creating a transcript? For this project, there definitely were other opportunities, and they were ones I had planned from the beginning. Therefore, I can use this knowledge to determine that the cost of collaboration, and all of that time dedicated to group work, is not worth it for this specific task.

The Goal of Collaboration Is Not Collaboration

The reason we collaborate is to achieve results we could not have without it. If an NBA point guard could win more games by not passing the ball and simply shooting it whenever he got the chance, that would be the best plan of action. However, that approach usually doesn't result in success for most teams (just ask Russell Westbrook), and the most successful teams are usually those that work together.

In the NBA, collaboration is required for success.

This is the same in the business world as well. The reason so many industries require collaboration is to enhance the work that is being done. In a capitalistic society, companies would not waste time and money for the sake of teamwork. They invest time and money when that teamwork has a measurable outcome.

We must think of the work in the classroom the same way. A teacher's time is limited and should not be wasted just because they want students to work together or because they've been told to. There must be a purpose to this work. When there is, collaboration is vital and can lead to incredible learning experiences (that's what this book is about, after all). But when it's not necessary, when it does more to hinder than help learning, it is best to just cut down branches and pick oranges by yourself.

Reflection

1. What do you think the strongest indicator is that a task should not be collaborative?
2. What is the difference between main course and dessert collaboration?
3. What should the goal of collaboration be?

Take Action

Identify any existing activities you already have planned that could be categorized as desserts. Now adapt or remove their collaboration aspect.

#CollaborativeClassroom

CHAPTER 10

WHAT ABOUT THE INTROVERTS?

Solitude matters, and for some people,
it's the air they breathe.

—Susan Cain, *Quiet*

My first teaching job was at a school designed and built for project-based learning. All of the classrooms had glass walls to emulate the open-floor concept made famous by Google and Facebook. Tables were round, and the chairs were flexible so students could always face each other. The mere idea of placing the flexible seating and rolling tables into rows was sacrilege.

Television monitors were placed all around the school for students to plug their computers into and project on the screens. The commons areas outside of classrooms were shaped like restaurant booths or high-top tables. Every square inch of the building was arranged for students to work together, designed to set the standard for collaborative classrooms, and I was determined to use it to its full extent.

I had rules in my class that chairs always had to stay at tables and could not be moved to the fringes of the classroom by themselves. The commons spaces beyond my room were for collaboration only, and any requests to use them by individuals were swiftly denied. Reading was done in groups, and all work was collaborative; every ounce of content taught in the class was done through discussion, conversation, and simulations. I took all of society's desires for more collaborative people, harnessed all of my disdain for a personal education experience that was strictly individual and even lonely, and grouped it with a school with millions of dollars in collaborative furniture to create the ultimate collaborative classroom.

About three months in, a huge portion of my students were wilting away in my innovative classroom. Kasey started getting sick before my class every day and would magically feel better in the nurse's office in time for her next class. Roger had minor panic attacks on a daily basis and would often put his head down on his desk for most of class. Dan's group members constantly complained to me about him not contributing to group work and said that he just sat quietly and would not speak when he was supposed to.

In less dramatic cases, many students just stopped looking like they were having any fun in my class, starting the class with energy and leaving every day drained and filled with anxiety. The culprit, blamed by students and parents over and over for this negative energy in my first classroom ever, was how much these students hated group work. My response was that these students just didn't know how to effectively collaborate yet. They spent most of their lives in traditional classrooms, and therefore they just needed time to adapt.

That wasn't the case, however, because no amount of experience collaborating or protocols or speeches from me helped these students. Many of my students seemed to love my class, but about a quarter of them loathed their time in my room.

Different Power Sources

If you likened my brain to a battery, the quickest way to charge it is to plug it into large groups of people. Whether it's leading, presenting to, or conversing with, I relish the opportunity to tap into the energy generated from large groups. It's why I gave the entire *I Have a Dream* speech to five hundred people from memory in the fourth grade; it's why I became a speaker and started presenting to professionals all over the world, and ultimately what led me to becoming a teacher. I get my energy from large groups of people.

When I started teaching and working with kids, I assumed everyone was energized the way I was. I imagined my students would be revitalized and thrive in constant community. This is what my policies of staying in the room and constant, face-to-face collaboration stemmed from. I thought I was serving my students in the best way possible. These were practices I thrive best with.

I am an extrovert.

The truth is, many innovations in education favor us extroverts. From the calls to abolish industrial-styled classrooms and replace them with flexible seating, to the rising prominence of project-based learning and designing entire curricula centered on group work, "innovative schools" are becoming a place where extroverts thrive. As a result, too many students who charge their batteries apart from the group, students who are less likely to speak up first in discussion and often want to separate from the masses, do not fit in with the format of an innovative class.

These students are often seen as problem cases in need of intervention because of their lack of contribution. Before I realized that introverts were in my classroom, or at least before I recognized how much my class favored the extroverts, I'd call parents and say things like, "Kasey is a great kid and does really strong work, but I just can't get her to talk enough in class." Or I would say to Kasey-the-Introvert, "I hardly heard a word from you today; why aren't you working with your group?"

For many introverts, sharing aloud in class is draining; sitting in groups with people and talking for an hour can be exhausting, and for many, it can even cause severe anxiety. Many of the aspects of a collaborative classroom will not come as easily for introverts, and yet half of all students (and people) are introverts.

Does this mean that introverts should be excused from collaboration and given the option to return to solely autonomous education?

Of course not! Whether a person is an introvert or extrovert, getting their energy from being with others or being alone, they need to learn the art of collaboration. This skill is too vital to make exceptions. However, this was my approach when I started teaching. I knew the vitality of teaching collaboration and did not care whether it was out of my students' comfort zones so long as they were learning and practicing the skill.

Kids like Kasey, Roger, and Dan were not learning how to collaborate when I was ignoring their tendency toward introversion. The class was too draining for them. The skills and attributes that come from being an introvert (and there are many) were repressed and ignored because the class was not made for them.

A collaborative classroom, even though it is rooted in regular contact and group work, needs to be tailored to all students, including the introvert. When introverts are considered and accommodated, collaboration thrives in a whole new way.

Collaboration Does Not Mean Constant Group Time

One of the myths of collaboration is that working together means always working together. For work to be collaborative, group members must always be conversing, brainstorming, and engaging in the same physical space. That's not collaboration. Collaboration means working together to solve a problem, and that is sometimes best done when group members have individual space in which to work. Collaboration requires that groups meet, often regularly, but that does not mean that autonomy is not vital.

Consider a symphony. Each member must rely on all of the others for the music and performance to be a success. Each member brings a unique set of skills to contribute, and whether playing violin or timpani, they must put aside any personal differences or conflicts to be in sync and create music that only an orchestra could create. A symphony orchestra requires strong collaboration, but most of a symphony musician's time is spent alone in practice, apart from the rest of the group. Concert violinist Leopold Auer says a musician should practice alone at least three hours a day. Musicians must master their parts before they can add to the collective. When a concertgoer is transfixed by the beauty and harmony of a symphony on a Saturday night, they are witnessing the product of thousands of hours of individual work.

A collaborative classroom has to recognize the value of individual work and practice. Some of the most effective problem solving occurs when group members are introduced to a problem or task as a collective, and then have time to solve portions of the task individually.

I had a conversation with Quynh Neutron,[1] a data engineer at Google. Quynh told me that collaboration is essential to the complex work she does for the tech giant. She sits at a desk in one of the famous open-floor-planned Google offices, surrounded by other professionals tasked with organizing and analyzing data. Specifically, Quynh works on teams to help data make sense for other teams at Google, and she has to listen to what these other teams need to help solve their problems. Her work is quintessentially collaborative. Even the motto for the division she works in at Google is "Lean on Each Other."

However, Quynh says that 70 percent of her time is spent alone at her desk. She convenes with her teams to become aware of the problems she has to solve and sometimes brainstorms with them, but she spends most of her time alone. In fact, Google even provides her and everyone else noise-canceling headphones to limit distractions during this work time.

We have to create this same type of space for our students. To do this, intentionally structure class time to allow for corporate and individual work. When a class is new to a collaborative culture, be specific with this time. You can say to a class, "You have five minutes to talk with your group about what needs to be accomplished today. When five minutes is up, you may begin working individually." This structure ensures that students do not spend the whole work time in conversation but also are creating. It also ensures that introverts have a manageable amount of time in discussion with their groups.

Rather than an hour of constant interaction that can be extremely draining, it's shorter and easier to cope with.

As the collaborative culture grows and evolves, you can become less stringent with this structure, and students can have more control of how they spend their time in group work. However, there always needs to be time for autonomy and moments for introverts to recharge alone.

Clinical Psychologist Ellen Hendriksen[2] writes in the *Quiet Revolution Blog* that introversion is something people are born with, whereas social anxiety is something people are taught. "Introversion is a part of your inherent personality—a from-the-womb, dyed-in-the-wool trait. And while those who are socially anxious also carry a genetic predisposition toward it," Hendrickson says, "there's more than just temperament at play. In an indelicate analogy, genetics loads the gun, but experience pulls the trigger." Introversion may come with its share of social anxiety, but that anxiety does not have to have the final say in a student's (and our own) collaborative success.

Introverts can be given the tools to thrive in groups, and after being in a collaborative classroom for a while, they can be conditioned to longer and more intense social interaction without the social anxiety. This is why I think it's perfectly okay to push introverts outside of their comfort zones and into collaborative groups even though that may not be their favorite learning environment. Nonetheless, introversion is a born trait, and the classroom has to accommodate it if our goal is for all students to succeed.

Take Advantage of the Strengths of Introverts

Perhaps one of the most important things we can do for introverts in a collaborative classroom is realize the value they can add to their groups. Although it may be easier for extroverted students to stand out in the classroom, this should not devalue introverts. A shift of mindset is required.

Susan Cain, the author of *Quiet: The Power of Introverts in a World That Can't Stop Talking*,[3] says that "Introverts have nervous systems that react more when there's just stuff going on around us." Cain says it "could be people, but it could also be bright lights and noise and so on. That means that we're feeling at our most alive and in our sweet spot when things are a little bit quieter and more mellow." In an interactive, busy, and sometimes loud classroom, people with this trait can get lost in the chaos. It's not that introverts are not gifted speakers, are not capable of contributing, or are even shy, it's that they process in a different way than extroverts.

This can often lead to thoughtful, measured responses. I personally like thinking out loud, throwing out as many ideas as I can and seeing what sticks. This admittedly can mean that some of the stuff that comes out of my mouth is not always intelligible at first. I might suggest four ideas before stumbling on the fifth one, which has merit. Introverts, on the other hand, usually spend time processing, measuring perspectives before contributing. When they do chime in, their words carry weight and value. We have to honor that as teachers and help students honor that in each other. Rather than seeing students as quiet or shy, recognize that they may be thinking deeply and are not yet ready to respond. It's too easy to think that these students do not know or have anything to contribute, when really they are just processing.

If conducting discussion, consider giving students discussion questions beforehand so they have time to process in quiet and are not forced to do so on the spot. This will lessen anxiety for introverts, but it also will ensure that they can contribute to their fullest potential.

Model to students what it looks like to give time for quiet thinking and reflection before responses. If you were going to have students turn and talk to each other after some type of demonstration or teaching, give thirty seconds for them to think first before responding. After their discussion, be explicit about why you gave that "thinking time." Ask how they could give that same kind of time to each other when working in groups. As an example, if a group of students were trying to figure out what image to use for a poster they were creating, instead of everyone just spit-balling ideas, they could say, "Let's think about this for two minutes and then share what we come up with." It's in those two minutes that introverts can compose their ideas and actually contribute rather than sitting quietly.

This is a strength of introverts that extroverts need to take advantage of as well. Just because extroverts might be more likely to draw inspiration externally and from interaction does not mean this is always the most valuable way. Sometimes just blurting out what is on your mind can get you in trouble (just ask my wife, who has lived with this extrovert for a decade). We can all benefit from time to process before responding.

This practice is transferable to the rest of life. When people realize each other's strengths and find ways to take advantage of them, they are helping ensure the best possible outcomes. They're taking advantage of what everyone brings to the table. In the workplace, if a manager who leads team meetings always gave thinking or process time to team members before soliciting responses, those responses would be so much stronger because the 50 percent of collaborators who are introverted would get the time they need to be successful.

The same is true with parenting, marriage, and friendships. We need to be aware of each other's personality types, what makes us tick, our strengths, and our weaknesses—the fact that we are all composed differently. This diversity is a strength in any community, but only if it is recognized and acted on. If I treated my son, who shows signs at the age of five of being an introvert, the same way as I treat my three-year-old daughter, who has no problem joining a crowd and leading the discussion, my son would not be as successful. If I give my son that processing time and allow him the quiet and space that he needs, he will be so much more likely to thrive.

A collaborative classroom needs to reflect this fact. It's still a learning environment founded on the power of the collective and using the creative power of people when they work together, but it also recognizes that this creative power is at its best when students also can work alone.

Reflection

1. How do collaborative activities sometimes disregard the needs of introverts?
2. How can introversion be used as an advantage in a collaborative classroom?
3. How can you create space in your classroom for extroverts and introverts to "recharge" in the ways that they need to?

WHEN WE COLLABORATE

When you sing with a group of people,
you learn how to subsume yourself
into a group consciousness . . . .
That's one of the great feelings—to
stop being me for a little while and to
become *us*. That way lays empathy,
the great social virtue.

—Brian Eno, composer

I n my fifth year as a teacher, I got very close to burning out.

In the first four years, I was determined to break the molds of the education system. I wanted to show that my students didn't need to sit in rows and listen to *me* talk all day to learn. In fact, I wanted to expose those old methods for what they really are: outdated and ineffective. I read too many *Forbes* articles about how businesses need people who can collaborate but aren't finding them. Too many students were graduating from high school lacking one of the most essential skills. Disgusting and divided political discourse was becoming the norm because even our leaders and representatives lacked this skill. If I wanted my students to thrive beyond their academic careers, my class would have to look different, because the old ways just weren't cutting it.

To meet this need, I developed a collaborative classroom and almost burned out.

The truth is, teaching collaboration is hard work. When students from a highly individual-focused environment are suddenly forced to work together—and not just the kind of together where everyone completes a slide and pastes it into the final presentation or the kind of together where one kid slacks while everyone else does the work— teaching collaboration is hard work.

When I started teaching, my focus was on the task at hand, whether it was discussion, a project, or students learning a specific piece of content. Collaboration was the format they completed the tasks in, but not the task in and of itself. I was using collaboration, but not teaching it. I didn't have all the structures and processes. I didn't give my students a system to hold each other accountable, manage their time, and deal with group conflict. I knew nothing about how to create effective groups and sometimes put high school freshmen into groups of eight. (*What was I thinking?*) My students didn't know how to solve problems, and I was constantly putting out fires, giving the same learning workshops ten times in a day, and dealing with parent phone calls about how their baby does not like the group they are in and how I *have* to move them.

Like trying to build a house on sand, I was innovating without a foundation for innovation. And after a while, the building collapsed. All of these issues that cause teachers to swear off group work were finally enough to make me curse it myself. The work of leading a collaborative classroom no longer seemed worth it.

Instead of outright quitting, I decided to make my classroom like the ones I sat in for the first sixteen years of my life. No more projects, no more inquiry; less student-led, more of me. I arranged the desks into neat rows, prepared slideshows during my prep hour, and made classroom management about keeping kids quiet while I stood in the front and lectured. For someone who likes to speak and be up front, I liked this new (old) way of teaching. I wasn't constantly having to move around the room or having to trust my students to get their work done. Now I controlled the class.

For a while, I liked this new format and how it was so much *easier for me* to operate in. My class became predictable: I do → students listen → then they demonstrate understanding. Like clockwork, and not nearly as messy as my class once was.

But it wasn't long before students started falling asleep at their desks. Their once inquisitive and curious eyes became blank as the minutes ticked by in my room. Every day, five minutes before the end of class, students discreetly started sliding their books into their backpacks, ready to make a mad break for the door when the bell rang.

Kids asked fewer questions and stopped geeking out with me about the content they were learning. They became needier and called me over to them every time they had a question, no matter how small their problem was.

And it wasn't long before I grew bored too. I got into this work to see students transform. Not to become just better readers and writers, but better thinkers and doers. The latter was no longer happening in my classroom, and in fact, neither was the former. I found that my disengaged, uninterested students were not learning the content any better when I explicitly taught it to them through direct instruction. I wasn't being the kind of teacher I had ever envisioned.

So I thought I'd try collaboration again, only this time I would emphasize this skill as much as anything else. I would spend time teaching my students to work together. I would build a collaborative culture that my students could thrive in. I would give them tools to work together and show them how to deal with conflict. I would resist every temptation to let students choose their own groups, no matter how much of a bad guy it made me. I would not make students collaborate anymore for the sake of collaboration, but instead I would only have my class do it when the task required it.

This was the beginning of a true collaborative classroom. There were bumps and obstacles—there always will be—but the light started shining behind my students' eyes. They began to own their learning and manage their time and work. The more they learned these processes and tools, the less they needed me to succeed. My students were equipped to deal with challenges and knew how to lean on each other to overcome them. Every day in the classroom was different now, and often unexpected. I was excited to come to work because I was eager to see what the day held.

And so were my students.

Collaboration was no longer just about getting students ready for the future; it was also dramatically enhancing their present. Simply put: people work better together.

We are wired for community. Whether introverted or extroverted, people are most comfortable when connected with others, sharing stories, emotions, and ideas with each other. When the classroom allows for this community to happen—*when it becomes a community*—when we stop making learning solely about the individual, but instead about everyone present, students engage. They thrive in a way the sit-and-get model would never allow them to. They learn that they need each other, that they do better when they work together, that there is not a problem they can't solve, whether it's long division, group conflict, or climate change, when they truly and meaningfully collaborate.

REFERENCES

Introduction

1. David F. Labaree. "Public Goods, Private Goods: The American Struggle over Educational Goals," *American Educational Research Journal*, 34, no. 1 (1997): 39, doi.org/10.2307/1163342.
2. Markku Allison, "Collaboration: Why Do We Need It? And, Uh, What Is It, Anyway?" *Work Design Magazine*, June 12, 2015, workdesign.com/2015/06/collaboration-why-do-we-need-it-and-uh-what-is-it-anyway/.
3. Simon Child and Stuart Shaw, "Collaboration in the 21st Century: Implications for Assessment," *Research Matters: A Cambridge Assessment Publication* 22 (Summer 2016): 17-22.

Additional Reading

Paul Petrone. "These Are the Skills of the Future, According to 39 Industry Experts." *LinkedIn: The Learning Blog*. September 25, 2017. learning.linkedin.com/blog/future-skills/these-are-the-skills-of-the-future—according-to-39-industry-exp?trk=lilblog_01-02-18_PULSE-Skills-Companies-Need-Most_tl&cid=70132000001AyziAAC.

"The Skills Companies Need Most in 2019—And How to Learn Them." *LinkedIn Learning*, learning.linkedin.com/blog/top-skills/the-skills-companies-need-most-in-2019—and-how-to-learn-them.

Karin Volo, "How Collaboration Is a Solution. *HuffPost*, February 6, 2014. huffpost.com/entry/how-collaboration-is-a-solution_b_4738169.

Chapter 1

1. Davis, Kathleen. "How Asana Built the Best Company Culture in Tech." *Fast Company* (March 31, 2017). fastcompany.com/3069240/how-asana-built-the-best-company-culture-in-tech.

Chapter 2

1. Elon Musk, "Making Humans a Multi-Planetary Species," *New Space*, 5, no. 2 (2017): 46–61, doi:10.1089/space.2017.29009.emu.
2. Loren Thompson, "Five Existential Challenges Facing Elon Musk's SpaceX," *Forbes*, (December 11, 2018), forbes.com/sites/lorenthompson/2018/12/11/five-existential-challenges-facing-elon-musks-spacex/#4643d611127d.
3. Sean O'Kane, "Neil DeGrasse Tyson: 'The Delusion Is Thinking That SpaceX Is Going to Lead the Space Frontier,'" *The Verge* (November 24, 2015), theverge.com/2015/11/24/9792854/neil-degrasse-tyson-interview-delusions-of-space-enthusiasts.

Additional Reading

Trevor Muir, "Most Common Struggles for Teachers When Assigning Group Work," TrevorMuir.com (August 27, 2019), trevormuir.com/new-blog-avenue/collaboration-struggles.

"How Structure Improves Your Child's Brain," *Psychology Today*, Sussex Publishers, psychologytoday.com/us/blog/think-better/201111/how-structure-improves-your-childs-brain.

Chapter 3

1. Barash, David P. "Are We Hard-Wired for War?" *The New York Times* (September 28, 2013). nytimes.com/2013/09/29/opinion/sunday/are-we-hard-wired-for-war.html.

2. "Pair Communication: Active-Listening Exercise." *School Reform Initiative*. schoolreforminitiative.org/download/pair-communication-active-listening-exercise/.

3. Rowling, J.K. *Harry Potter and the Sorcerer's Stone*. New York: Scholastic, 1998. nytimes.com/2013/09/29/opinion/sunday/are-we-hard-wired-for-war.html.

Chapter 4

1. Alison Doyle, "How Often Do People Change Jobs?" *The Balance Careers* (January 29, 2019), thebalancecareers.com/how-often-do-people-change-jobs-2060467.

2. "Freelancers Union and Upwork release new study revealing insights into the almost 54 million people freelancing in America." *Upwork.com*. (2015), upwork.com/press/2015/10/01/freelancers-union-and-upwork-release-new-study-revealing-insights-into-the-almost-54-million-people-freelancing-in-america/.

3. Rob Waugh, "Why adaptability is key to success?" *The Telegraph* (London; December 10, 2018), telegraph.co.uk/connect/better-business/business-solutions/adaptability-in-the-workplace/.

4. Lucas Miller, "9 Reasons Talented Millennials Get Fired." *Entrepreneur Magazine* (December 20, 2017), entrepreneur.com/article/305852.

5. Lynn Taylor, Tame Your Terrible Office Tyrant: How to Manage Childish Boss Behavior and Thrive in Your Job (Hoboken, NJ: John Wiley & Sons), 2009.

6. Helene Lerner, The Confidence Myth: Why Women Undervalue Their Skills and How to Get Over It (Oakland: Berrett-Koehler Publishers), 2015.

7. Dweck, Carol S.. *Mindset: The New Psychology Of Success*. New York: Ballantine Books, 2008. Print.

8. Barney Saltzberg, *Beautiful Oops!* (New York: Workman), 2010.

9. Peter H. Reynolds and Maria Liatis, *The Dot.* (Fairfax, VA: Library Ideas, LLC), 2019.

10. Gary M. Rubinstein and Mark Pett, *The Girl Who Never Makes Mistakes,* (Naperville, IL: Sourcebooks), 2011.

11. Scott O'Dell, Stefani Paine, Joseph Bruchac, and Tomiko Higa. *Island of the Blue Dolphins: and Related Readings* (Sacramento, CA: Clearinghouse for Specialized Media & Technology), 2003.

12. Christopher Paul Curtis, *The Watsons Go to Birmingham: 1963* (New York: Yearling Book), 2013.

13. Louis Sachar, *Holes* (New York: Farrar, Straus and Giroux), 2018.

Chapter 6

1. Patrick R. Laughlin, *Group Problem Solving* (Princeton, NJ: Princeton University Press), 2011.

2. Lynda Gratton and Tamara J. Erickson, "Eight Ways to Build Collaborative Teams." *Harvard Business Review* (November 2007), hbr.org/2007/11/eight-ways-to-build-collaborative-teams.

Chapter 7

1. Harry McCracken, "Google Glass: An Eyes-on Evaluation." *Time* (February 2013), techland.time.com/2013/02/22/google-glass-an-eyes-on-evaluation/.

2. John Brandon, "Was Google Glass the Worst Tech Gadget Ever Invented?" *Inc.com,* (January 15, 2015), inc.com/john-brandon/was-google-glass-the-worst-tech-gadget-ever-invented.html.

3. Mark Payne, How to Kill a Unicorn: How the World's Hottest Innovation Factory Builds Bold Ideas That Make It to Market (New York: Crown Business), 2014.

4. Marcial Losada and Emily Heaphy. "The Role of Positivity and Connectivity in the Performance of Business Teams: A Nonlinear Dynamics Model." *American Behavioral Scientist* 47, no. 6 (2004): 740-765. doi.org/10.1177/0002764203260208.

Chapter 8

1. "Mobile Fact Sheet," *Pew Research Center,* pewinternet.org/fact-sheet/mobile.
2. Scott Mautz, "What Job Skill Is Most Lacking in the U.S.? LinkedIn CEO Jeff Weiner Has a Surprising Answer." *Inc.com.* (April 23, 2018).
3. David S. Yeager, et al. "Boring But Important: A Self-Transcendent Purpose for Learning Fosters Academic Self-Regulation." *Journal of Personality and Social Psychology,* 107, no. 4 (2014): 559-580, doi: 10.1037/a0037637.
4. C. S. Hulleman, O. Godes, B. L. Hendricks, and J. M. Harackiewicz, "Enhancing interest and performance with a utility value intervention," *Journal of Educational Psychology,* 102, no. 4 (2010): 880-895, dx.doi.org/10.1037/a0019506.

Chapter 10

1. Cain, Susan. Quiet: The Power of Introverts in a World That Can't Stop Talking. New York: Crown Publishers, 2012.
2. Neutron, Quynh. "Interview With Quynh Neutron." Interview by Trevor Muir (April 5, 2019).
3. "The 4 Differences Between Introversion and Social Anxiety." *Quiet Revolution* (May 20, 2016). quietrev.com/the-4-differences-between-introversion-and-social-anxiety/.

MORE FROM

DAVE **B**URGESS
Consulting, inc.

Since 2012, DBCI has been publishing books that inspire and equip educators to be their best. For more information on our DBCI titles or to purchase bulk orders for your school, district, or book study, visit **DaveBurgessconsulting.com/DBCIbooks**.

More from the *Like a PIRATE*™ Series

Teach Like a PIRATE by Dave Burgess

eXPlore Like a Pirate by Michael Matera

Learn Like a Pirate by Paul Solarz

Play Like a Pirate by Quinn Rollins

Run Like a Pirate by Adam Welcome

Lead Like a PIRATE™ Series

Lead Like a PIRATE by Shelley Burgess and Beth Houf

Balance Like a Pirate by Jessica Cabeen, Jessica Johnson, and Sarah Johnson

Lead beyond Your Title by Nili Bartley

Lead with Appreciation by Amber Teamann and Melinda Miller

Lead with Culture by Jay Billy

Lead with Literacy by Mandy Ellis

Leadership & School Culture

Culturize by Jimmy Casas

Escaping the School Leader's Dunk Tank by Rebecca Coda and Rick Jetter

From Teacher to Leader by Starr Sackstein

The Innovator's Mindset by George Couros

Kids Deserve It! by Todd Nesloney and Adam Welcome

Let Them Speak by Rebecca Coda and Rick Jetter

The Limitless School by Abe Hege and Adam Dovico

The Pepper Effect by Sean Gaillard

The Principled Principal by Jeffrey Zoul and Anthony McConnell

Relentless by Hamish Brewer

The Secret Solution by Todd Whitaker, Sam Miller, and Ryan Donlan

Start. Right. Now. by Todd Whitaker, Jeffrey Zoul, and Jimmy Casas

Stop. Right. Now. by Jimmy Casas and Jeffrey Zoul

They Call Me "Mr. De" by Frank DeAngelis

Unmapped Potential by Julie Hasson and Missy Lennard

Word Shift by Joy Kirr

Your School Rocks by Ryan McLane and Eric Lowe

Technology & Tools

50 Things You Can Do with Google Classroom by Alice Keeler and Libbi Miller

50 Things to Go Further with Google Classroom by Alice Keeler and Libbi Miller

140 Twitter Tips for Educators by Brad Currie, Billy Krakower, and Scott Rocco

Block Breaker by Brian Aspinall

Code Breaker by Brian Aspinall

Google Apps for Littles by Christine Pinto and Alice Keeler

Master the Media by Julie Smith

Shake Up Learning by Kasey Bell

Social LEADia by Jennifer Casa-Todd

Teaching Math with Google Apps by Alice Keeler and Diana Herrington

Teachingland by Amanda Fox and Mary Ellen Weeks

Teaching Methods & Materials

All 4s and 5s by Andrew Sharos

Boredom Busters by Katie Powell

The Classroom Chef by John Stevens and Matt Vaudrey

Copyrighteous by Diana Gill

Ditch That Homework by Matt Miller and Alice Keeler

Ditch That Textbook by Matt Miller

Don't Ditch That Tech by Matt Miller, Nate Ridgway,
and Angelia Ridgway

EDrenaline Rush by John Meehan

Educated by Design by Michael Cohen, The Tech Rabbi

The EduProtocol Field Guide by Marlena Hebern
and Jon Corippo

The EduProtocol Field Guide: Book 2 by Marlena Hebern
and Jon Corippo

Instant Relevance by Denis Sheeran

LAUNCH by John Spencer and A.J. Juliani

Make Learning MAGICAL by Tisha Richmond

Pure Genius by Don Wettrick

The Revolution by Darren Ellwein and Derek McCoy

Shift This! by Joy Kirr

Spark Learning by Ramsey Musallam

Sparks in the Dark by Travis Crowder and Todd Nesloney

Table Talk Math by John Stevens

The Wild Card by Hope and Wade King

The Writing on the Classroom Wall by Steve Wyborney

Inspiration, Professional Growth & Personal Development

Be REAL by Tara Martin

Be the One for Kids by Ryan Sheehy

The Coach ADVenture by Amy Illingworth

Creatively Productive by Lisa Johnson

Educational Eye Exam by Alicia Ray

The EduNinja Mindset by Jennifer Burdis

Empower Our Girls by Lynmara Colón and Adam Welcome

Finding Lifelines by Andrew Grieve and Andrew Sharos

The Four O'Clock Faculty by Rich Czyz

How Much Water Do We Have? by Pete and Kris Nunweiler

P Is for Pirate by Dave and Shelley Burgess

A Passion for Kindness by Tamara Letter

The Path to Serendipity by Allyson Apsey

Sanctuaries by Dan Tricarico

The SECRET SAUCE by Rich Czyz

Shattering the Perfect Teacher Myth by Aaron Hogan

Stories from Webb by Todd Nesloney

Talk to Me by Kim Bearden

Teach Better by Chad Ostrowski, Tiffany Ott, Rae Hughart, and Jeff Gargas

Teach Me, Teacher by Jacob Chastain

TeamMakers by Laura Robb and Evan Robb

Through the Lens of Serendipity by Allyson Apsey

The Zen Teacher by Dan Tricarico

Children's Books

Beyond Us by Aaron Polansky

Cannonball In by Tara Martin

Dolphins in Trees by Aaron Polansky

I Want to Be a Lot by Ashley Savage

The Princes of Serendip by Allyson Apsey

Zom-Be a Design Thinker by Amanda Fox

BRING TREVOR MUIR TO YOUR SCHOOL OR DISTRICT

Trevor's first passion is exciting students to become enthusiastic, engaged, and impassioned learners. His second love is inspiring others to do the same.

Using storytelling, giving examples from his own career, and sharing proven and effective practices, Trevor inspires educators and other professionals to lead a more compelling and engaging classroom and life. In the past few years, Trevor has traveled the globe giving keynotes and workshops, including leading the Design Expedition at Fontys University in the Netherlands, talking to PhD students in Bogota, Colombia, and brainstorming with elementary teachers in rural Iowa. Trevor offers the perspective of an author, speaker, project-based learning expert, and most importantly, a classroom teacher, to help teachers find more ways to engage their students and transform their classrooms.

Popular Messages from Trevor Muir

- Make Learning Epic: Teaching With the Power of Story
- Epic Project Based Learning
- Let's Collaborate: Using Collaborative Learning For Effective, Engaging, and Unforgettable Learning
- Launching Rockets—Making Connections with Challenging Students
- Stop Calling Them Soft Skills! (Because there is nothing soft about getting fired)

What People Are Saying about Trevor Muir

"This was one of the best keynotes I've ever seen. Trevor made us laugh; he made us cry. And I left with tools to really put his ideas into practice in my own classroom."

"Every teacher wants to have the kind of impact that Trevor is talking about. Every teacher wants to create the kind of experiences in the classroom that he's laying out. Today my staff and I were learning how to do that."

"Trevor is a dynamic speaker who fuses humor, thoughtful insights, and powerful storytelling into his sessions and keynotes. He understands what truly matters and conveys it in a way that is powerful and approachable. Audience members leave feeling both inspired and empowered."

"Trevor really set the inspirational tone that teachers need to kick off the school year with energy and motivation."

Connect

🌐 trevormuir.com

✉ trevor@trevormuir.com

🐦 @trevormuir

📘 The Epic Classroom- Trevor Muir

📷 @theepicclassroom

ABOUT THE AUTHOR

Trevor is a teacher, author, international speaker, and project-based learning expert. At the heart of Trevor's work is the conviction that *every student* has the potential for greatness, and *every teacher* can be equipped to unlock that potential.

He is the author of *The Epic Classroom: How to Boost Engagement, Make Learning Memorable, and Transform Lives*, a book about using the power of story to make learning engaging and unforgettable. Trevor is a professor at Grand Valley State University, a former faculty member for the Buck Institute for Education, and is one of the Andrew Gomez Dream Foundation educators. His writing has been featured in the *Huffington Post*, *EdWeek*, and regularly on *WeAreTeachers*. He gave a TEDx Talk titled, "School Should Take Place in the Real World," at TEDxSanAntonio. Trevor's Facebook page, The Epic Classroom, has inspiring videos for educators that have been viewed over 26 million times.

Trevor and his wife, Alli, live in Grand Rapids, Michigan, with their two children and a golden retriever.

CPSIA information can be obtained
at www.ICGtesting.com
Printed in the USA
JSHW031548140522
25852JS00004B/21